NORTHWEST GLORY DAYS

FUNNY AND FORGOTTEN TRUE STORIES, ADVENTURES AND INCIDENTS FROM THE YOUNG AND EXCITING NORTHWEST

By Marge Davenport

NORTHWEST GLORY DAYS

Published By: **PADDLEWHEEL PRESS**
15100 S.W. 109th
Tigard, Oregon 97223 USA

Printed in the United States of America

Library of Congress Cataloging in Publication Data
Davenport, Marge E., date

ISBN No. 0-938274-02-3
Library of Congress Catalog Card No.

FOREWORD

Researching the early history of the Pacific Northwest is fun and exciting. In the old manuscripts, letters, newspaper clippings, diaries and recollections are tales of intrigue, humor, long-forgotten phenomena, and mind-boggling drama.

As these many tales come to light from dusty volumes, it is more and more apparent that the Pacific Northwest is the forgotten, neglected, and largely unsung American frontier.

We all learned about Pocahontas, but who ever heard of the Indian Princess of the Rogue River who risked her life for the man she loved and consequently saved a whole white settlement?

There was a Northwest hostage crisis in 1851 as serious at the time as the Iranian crisis of our time. Who remembers the time Mother Nature spawned a sudden and violent half-hour storm off the Oregon-Washington Coast that drowned more than 325 fishermen on May 4, 1880.

As Northwest settlers and settlements fought for survival and growth in the early days there was skullduggery and conniving. Competition was fierce on all fronts as men became quick millionaires or were gunned down in range disputes. But lots of funny things happened, too, and often a good sense of humor saved the day.

Learning about the Northwest's 'glory days' has made the present day Northwest an ever more fascinating place to live for me — I hope it does for you, too.

Marge Davenport

FOR THE RECORD

A book about the early Northwest would not be possible without the help of many people. I am especially appreciative for the help of many librarians in various Northwest libraries; to the staff of the Oregon Historical Society library and to the staffs of other historical societies and foundations for their assistance.

Special thanks is also due Barney McPhillips, Sr., whose stories of the early days deserve a separate volume; to Lydge Cady and Baxter Hubbard, who helped with editing; to my daughter Janet Little who helped with some of the research; and to Artist Tom Robel, who helped with illustrations. I am most appreciative to them and to Artisan Typesetting for their patience and expertise.

About the author

Marge Davenport & friend

Marge Davenport is a native of the Northwest with many interests and accomplishments.

She holds a commercial pilot's license, an Oregon real estate license, has owned and run her own flower shops and has traveled widely about the world, always returning to the Northwest proclaiming it 'the best place of all to live and enjoy life.'

Ms. Davenport's writing, which is her first love, has won her many awards, including a presidential citation. She was a staff writer for the Oregon Journal, specializing in medicine and science, and is amember of the National Association of Science Writers. She has been a contributor to Science Digest, Field and Stream, Ladies Home Journal, Reader's Digest, Dalles Times Herald and many professional publications.

Always interested in Northwest history, Ms. Davenport's reseach has taken her to large, small and private libraries from California to Canada.

An enthusiastic outdoors person, Ms. Davenport's other interests include a 'menagerie of cats, dogs and horses,' five daughters, and all kinds of Northwest activities. She does watercolors, swims, fishes, canoes, hikes and backpacks.

Horse racing was one of the most popular pastimes in early Northwest. Often the main street of town was the race track and the bets were heavy.

Proud conductors on Portland's first electric cars worked 16 hour shifts for $2.15 per day. Price to ride across Willamette River was five cents, but rail service was financial success because it also cost five cents to walk across bridge.

Early Days Were Glory Days

In 1805, only a little more than 175 years ago, the Pacific Northwest was a wilderness. There were no white settlers, only Indians who lived off the land and the bounties of the sea.

Before this, ships from many countries had touched the shores of Puget Sound and the Columbia River, but there were no permanent settlements, and the land was unexplored.

That year, 1805, the first white explorers, Lewis and Clark, sent by the President of the United States, made their historic overland trip to the Pacific Ocean. Their report when they returned east created only slight interest in the wild Northwest.

But the Hudson Bay Company of England, who had already established a profitable fur trading business in Canada was interested in the reports of this land rich in fur-bearing animals. They pushed west and established the first trading posts in the Northwest.

Firmly entrenched and well-financed and managed, the Hudson Bay Company ruled the Northwest for the next 30 years under the firm hand of Factor McLoughlin. A few Americans, John Jacob Astor and later Nathaniel Wyeth, also hoping to cash in on the fur trade, tried to gain a foothold, but were not successful.

When American missionaries began arriving at the Hudson Bay post at Vancouver on the Columbia River, McLoughlin encouraged them to settle south of the Columbia. The Marcus Whitmans chose to establish a mission at Ft. Walla Walla. The Whitmans were massacred by the Indians they came to save, and other missions struggled without much success.

About 1842, adventurers and a few settlers lured by stories of free land and great opportunity began to arrive. Quite a few Hudson Bay men retired and settled on land.

These were followed by more settlers, many of them tired of the rigors of the mid-west. Without realizing the hardships they would suffer, many loaded their families and possessions into wagons and set out on the Oregon Trail. By 1843, the great westward migration was on.

Those who survived the overland trip joined those who made the long arduous passage by sailing ship to the Northwest. On the way, both groups found hardships almost beyond belief, and when they arrived they faced a struggle for survival and many difficulties.

Disgruntled Indians, realizing they were losing their land to the whites, were a constant problem. Many rogues and outlaws had been attracted to the country, along with the serious minded farmers and merchants. There was no law and gambling, saloons and prostitution flourished in the fast-growing settlements. There were horse thieves and stage-coach robbers.

In some places, citizens took law and order into their own hands and posses and vigilantes sometimes made quick, fatal and unfortunate decisions.

The discovery of gold in California, followed by discoveries of the glittering metal in parts of the Northwest and in the Klondike, quickly changed the face and the pace of Northwest growth. Many Northwest settlers dropped everything and left for the California mines. Thousands poured into the Northwest to seek quick riches on the river banks and in the mines here and in British Columbia. Gold fever was rampant and wild little tent cities sprang up. Some persons got rich, but many went back to their homes poorer than when they left.

These and the subsequent years when the settlers set about to establish government, tame the wilderness, build boats, roads and railroads, were exciting times in the Northwest. Heroes were made; men became millionaires overnight, and some lost fortunes just as fast. And lots of funny things happened. The rugged Northwest spawned characters and story tellers; it had its heroines, too, and villains emerged.

These were the Northwest's Glory Days.

CONTENTS

COLORFUL CHARACTERS

SOME NORTHWEST HUMOR

THE WAY IT WAS

GETTING THERE

SKULLDUGGERY & CONNIVING

DID WOMEN WIN NORTHWEST?

MOTHER NATURE'S HAND

INDIANS WERE FIRST

PLACES & HAPPENINGS

HEALTHY MEDICINE?

AROUND THE NORTHWEST

COLORFUL CHARACTERS

Stronger Than Iron

The "strong men" of the Northwest continue to live in legend.

Washington State has its "Iron Man of the Hoh," a homesteader on the Olympic Peninsula's rain forest area, who was said to be a man of superhuman strength. His name was Huseldunk, and one of the stories about him tells how he carried a heavy iron kitchen range into his homestead in the mountains on his back. When asked if the range wasn't terribly heavy, he is said to have replied that he didn't mind the weight of the stove, but that the sack of flour that he had put in the over kept shifting around and caused him a little problem.

Oregon's strong man was Israel Fisk Eddy, who lived from 1824 to 1911. He was six foot seven inches tall, and was reported to be very powerful. He weighed 250 pounds and was said to have had to stoop to enter an ordinary door.

There are many tales about Israel's great strength. One witness wrote that he saw him lift the wheel of a loaded hay wagon clear so it could be pulled out of the mud.

It was also reported that Israel could put a heavy steel spike between his fingers and slam it down and that the spike would bend to the shape of his fingers. The grandson of James Eddy, who fought in the Revolutionary War, Israel came to Oregon in 1870 and settled in the area which was later named for him, Eddyville. He built a sawmill and a grist mill, and a dam on the Yaquina River to supply power to his mills.

Israel also built a grocery store and planted a large apple orchard. He was very fond of festive occasions and entertained at these affairs by playing a hand organ.

Upstairs over the grocery store, he curtained off rooms which he rented to overnight travelers going between Corvallis and the coast. On Saturday night, the curtains would come down and a dance would attract persons from all around the country. People would arrive in wagons, put the kids to bed in the wagon and spend the night in festivities. Usually there was liquor and when fights occurred, Israel broke them up by taking each of the combatants by the back of the neck, escorting them outside and dumping them in the watering trough.

In 1908, Israel was 84 years old and still going strong. He wore a coonskin cap, had a booming voice and carried an ear trumpet. Arriving at a party where someone inquired how his ailment (malaria?) was, Israel replied that he had cured it by mistakenly taking a swig of piano polish when he thought he was taking his medicine. He died at 87.

Courtesy Oregon Historical Society

Camping Debt Collector

In the early 1900's, the Northwest had a unique debt collector who was amazingly successful in his business.

James McDonald, "collector of good and bad debts," said he went into the collection business initially to collect some bad debts owed to him. Then a grocer induced him to collect some debts for him, and McDonald was so successful that he made a new career out of debt collecting.

His debt collecting method consisted of a large sign painted on a piece of cloth and worn across his chest by the old, gray-bearded man. It said:

"Collector of good & bad debts. Moody says, 'If you ever expect to gain heaven, you must pay your debts.' I shall camp here until you pay!"

On stubborn cases, McDonald also added a horse bell to his collecting tools. In addition to donning his sign and "camping" with the person owing the debt, McDonald rang the horse bell if he was being ignored.

"The bell generally brings them out," he declared.

Born in 1823 on Prince Edward Island, McDonald went to New Brunswick when he was 22 years old and engaged in the lumber business. In 1850, he sailed for California and eventually landed at the mouth of the Umpqua River in Oregon. There he did day work until he got enough money to buy a pack mule.

With the mule he started doing commercial packing from Scottsburg to Yoncalla, 35 miles over mountainous trail. Soon he had enough money to buy more mules. By 1856, he had a sizeable outfit and was packing for the government during the Indian War.

Then, at the Massacre at the Cascades on March 26, 1856, McDonald's pack train was captured by the Indians and he barely escaped to The Dalles with his life. He filed a claim for $10,000 against the government, but 39 years later when he was interviewed in Portland it was unpaid and still pending.

After his pack train was captured, McDonald went to farming and he was successful until the severe winter of 1861 wiped out his livestock. Once again, he started over. Then in 1886, he came to Portland to collect numerous bad debts that he said were owed him. He said if he could collect what was due him he would be worth $200,000, instead of the $12,000 which he held in property.

During his years as a bill collector in Portland, McDonald's reputation spread and he became quite famous. He had one shortcoming, however, he said. He generally gave away more than he made.

"When people put on a good deal of style and are able to pay their bills, but will not, then I try to collect with my little badge. In most cases it has the desired effect," he said.

McDonald was arrested twice during his collection career. Once on complaint of a clothier who became annoyed when McDonald stood in front of his store with his badge and bell. The amused judge dismissed the charges after listening to the case. Another time a restaurant owner complained, but failed to appear in court. ❖

Hathaway's Smart Dog

One of the greatest story tellers that the Northwest has produced was an early day mail carrier on the Rogue River in Southwest Oregon.

His name was Hathaway Jones and he became a legend in the Rogue country because his incredible tales were skillfully woven around the everyday things of life, and he seemed to have an endless supply of these tall tales.

Carrying the mail up and down the steep trail that follows the Rogue was no easy task. Jones carried it in all kinds of weather with a canvas bag slung over his back, and when he arrived at one of the scattered cabins, he dumped the contents of the mail bag out on the floor and told stories while the folks sorted out their mail. Needless to say, the homesteaders along the river were always glad to see Jones coming, not only because he brought the mail, but because he also brought some fun and entertainment into their rather lonely and isolated lives.

As his fame spread, Hathaway Jones stories were told and retold up and down the river, and even today, if you make the white water trip down the Rogue you can pretty well be certain that you will hear a Hathaway Jones tale somewhere along the way.

Jones was born in 1870. He started carrying mail on the long and lonely trail along the Rogue in 1898. A tall, thin man with a harelip, Jones did not let his speech impediment bother him or make him self conscious.

One of Jones' most famous stories was about the dog that was the smartest dog ever, he said. This dog took a stick in its mouth and backed into the river so that all the fleas worked up to its head and then they jumped onto the stick. The dog then discarded the stick and got rid of all his fleas.

Another of Hathaway's stories, often repeated, was about a big rock along the trail where the river ran through a steep canyon. Jones said he always wondered what would happen if he could push the precariously balanced rock into the river, so one day he gave it a mighty shove.

Down it went, trees snapping off in its path. He saw it go up the other side of the canyon and it had picked up so much momentum that it went further up the other side than where he was standing. Then, instead of stopping, he saw the rock coming back down up toward where he was standing.

"I jumped on my horse and grabbed my pack mule and we skeedaddled. I was afraid it was coming right up over the ridge where I had been standing."

Jones said he didn't get back to that canyon for 20 years, but when he did he heard a little noise, like a rattlesnake makes.

"So I kinda sneaked up to see what it was. There was a great big chute up both sides of the canyon worn smooth and polished and right down at the bottom of it was this little stone, no bigger than a marble, and it was still coming up one side and going back down and up the other side. That was five years ago, there's probably nothing left of it by now."

Hathaway Jones was still packing mail when he died in 1937. His saddle turned and he was thrown off and hit his head on a rock. He is buried in Illahe.

Earliest Promoter

John Ledyard, a native of Connecticut, was a man whose name has not been linked with the exploration and settlement of the Northwest, but he, perhaps as much as anyone, is at least indirectly responsible for Northwest exploration and development.

In 1778, Ledyard made the trip to the West Coast of America with Captain Cook. Returning home, he then joined the British Navy because of his love of adventure. However, because of his experience with Cook, he deserted from a man-of-war in Long Island Sound and began traveling to the major moneyed centers of the United States to try to interest men of means in sending more expeditions to the West Coast.

He was coldly received in most places, and in New York he was treated as a dreamer with a visionary mind when he talked about the riches of the fur trade and the possibilities for settlement on the West Coast. In Philadelphia, he was given a better welcome, and Bostonians were impressed, but decided there were too many risks involved. Because of tales of hostile Indians, they feared that not enough men of courage could be found to risk the hazards of the sea, disease and the Indian hordes. Besides, there was the risk of investing in such hazardous explorations.

Discouraged, Ledyard went to Europe to try to find venture capital there. Thomas Jefferson, representing the American Confederacy in Paris, was sympathetic and gave Ledyard's idea support, but once again he failed to raise the necessary money.

Accepting the advice of Jefferson, Ledyard then started across Europe and Asia with the purpose of reaching the shores of the Pacific Coast and exploring. He was captured by Russian Officers in Siberia and expelled. Following this, he entered the services of African exploration, where he perished.

But Ledyard's enthusism for America's West Coast was not forgotten, and the world owes its first knowledge of the resources of Oregon and the Northwest to Cook's expedition and Ledyard's dedicated campaign to publicize it.

A few years later the Bostonians Robert Gray and John Kendrick made their voyage of 1787 to the area, and in 1805, when Thomas Jefferson became president, he remembered the conversations he had with Ledyard and sent Lewis and Clark to the Pacific Coast. ❖

Pioneer Philosopher

An early Northwest man whose name is not carved in marble, nor sung in history books, left some philosophical throughts and did some memorable things that perhaps should give him a place in Northwest legend.

He was E.H. Collis, and statistics show that he was assistant secretary of Pacific Marine Iron Works, treasurer of Scio Logging and Lumber Company and treasurer of Columbia Chemical Company.

More importantly Collis was also an enthusiastic outdoorsperson and a pursuer of knowledge.

His walking tours took him over most of the Northwest and he was an ardent collector. But he also was always buying books for children as he traveled, although he had no children of his own. He presented these books to other children because he thought all children should be encouraged to read and seek knowledge.

Collis explained his life philosophy — "It is not the thing that costs the most money that brings the most pleasure, but it is doing the thing that leaves a glow in your heart through giving someone else unexpected pleasure that counts."

He also is credited with saying, "Most of us can get more money, but none of us can get more time. Our days are numbered, and yet we go on wasting what life is made of — merely existing instead of living.

"Many people are slaves of the treadmill. We keep our eyes on the ground and our thoughts on things of minor importance, ignoring the really worthwhile things and allowing the things that make life worht living to pass by unused and unenjoyed."   ❖

Early Days at Maryhill were exciting ones, according to 88-year-old Mrs. Lund who was teenager there in 1915. VIP's and European Royalty were often guests.

Sam's Bluing Keg

Sam Hill, who built the famous Maryhill Museum on the Columbia River, was not the railroad magnate, but was from another family and was the adopted son of Jim Hill, the railroad man. Sam was adopted by Jim when he married Jim's daughter, and he took the name of Hill.

This information, not recorded in historical documents turned up by researchers by Ann Lund, 88 years old, who now lives in Raymond, Wash. Mrs. Lund, who was 15 years old at the time, lived in the hotel there owned by Sam Hill with her family who managed the hotel at the time Maryhill was being built.

Here is the interesting story of Maryhill as Mrs. Lund recalls it:

"Sam Hill was a fine person, make no mistake on that. He wanted to do something to improve the land and help people realize what a beautiful location it was, and that much could be done to make it a really unusual and desirable place to live.

"He tried very hard to show what could be done there and it cost him lots of money, too. He brought so many guests from Europe and from all over the United States," Mrs. Lund recalls.

"He used to stand on the porch at the hotel which was also on the hill and watch the sunset over Mt. Hood, and would say to me that nothing anywhere he had traveled could compare to that beautiful mountain sunset. He said he hoped to be buried in a vault under the hill from the hotel where the sun shone on it.

"It was sad to know that after his death he did not get his wish."

In answer to questions about conditions at Maryhill when she lived there, Mrs. Lund says her family came there before the hotel was complete.

"There were about eight apartments upstairs, with a large bath, and shower on the ground floor, along with a large kitchen, dining room, office and lobby. There was a porch around three sides of the hotel. The dining room was large and there was a large ice room for keeping food.

"D. B. Hill had a post office in a separate building, which also had an apartment and bath. There was also a stable to care for Maryhill's driving team. They were trained high-steppers and beautiful animals, sent to Maryhill from St. Paul. The boy who cared for them was a Washington State College student.

"An experimental farm of 12 acres was located 12 miles from the hotel, and beautiful grapes were raised there. The purpose was to prove to interested buyers that one could raise anything in the area. One bunch of grapes weighed 12 pounds.

"Among problems with the area were the wind and sand storms. When grass seed was planted around the hotel to make a nice lawn, it was blown across the gully on the hill and came up over there and the hill was nice and green, but there wasn't a spear at the hotel yard.

"One of Sam's guests at the hotel at one time was a lady who wore a pant skirt and we all saw her go out to the fence around the hotel to go to the stable and she just took a run and leaped right over the fence wall. You can imagine what a shock that was 73 years ago. It became a widespread story as it was so shocking.

"Another time, we had a Duke from Europe as a guest. I was doing the room service at the time and when he set his shoes out in the hall to be cleaned it made me so angry that I carried them to the other end of the hotel and he had to go find them.

"Washington State was dry at the time, but Maryhill always had plenty to drink. A keg marked bluing or vinegar was kept in the storeroom by the kitchen door.

"Sam was a fine person and treated me with respect. I admired him very much. He never brought his wife Mary to the hotel, nor his mother-in-law either, as they were too ill to be taken out in public.

"When the castle was built, bars were put on the windows upstairs to protect these two women from jumping out of their rooms, because of their mental condition. However, plans were evidently changed and they were never brought to the place.

"I can't say if Sam intended to live there. I doubt it as he was used to hobnobbing with a class of folk who had money. The workmen stayed at Maryhill when working there if they did not live close by."

Mrs. Lund moved to New York before the castle was complete, but she remembers the stories told at the time about Sam Hill's origin. He was said to come from a poor family, but was a nice young man and a ticket agent working in the station of Hill and Harriman Railroad, and was promised to be the heir of Jim's as the older man had no sons and a mentally defective girl.

"It was said Sam married the daughter, Mary, to get out of the poor way of life, and that is the only reason I know, but maybe he had other ones," Mrs. Lund says.

She adds that "Columbus" was the name of the settlement and hotel site down by the river and the railroad track, and that the name Maryhill applied only to the complex on the hill.

"Sam had the Columbus Land Company, and hoped to sell land to folks who would love it like he did. However, there were lots of rattlesnakes and the wild horses would come right down to the hotel yard at times."

Recalling life at Maryhill while she was still there, Mrs. Lund remembers many good times — a dance held for her when the hotel was finished. ❖

Many fortunes were made on waterways of early Northwest because this was main means of transportation for many years.

Paddlewheel Millionaire

When he was 14 years old, Jacob Kamm found himself alone in America, jobless and friendless and with ten cents in his pocket. Before he died, Kamm was one of the Northwest's richest men.

Born in Switzerland, his father took him at age 8 and set out for the Coast of France. Kamm remembered the trip well because all they had to eat twice a day during the long trek was brown bread and pork fat — "just clean fat, no lean about it," he recalled.

When they reached the coast, they boarded a ship for a six month sailing trip that ended in New Orleans. Then the pair continued to St. Louis where the father engaged in farming and ran a grist mill.

When he was 13, it was decided that young Jacob should begin an apprenticeship on a New Orleans newspaper. He had not been there long when he received word that his father had died of yellow fever. Jacob went back to St. Louis, but he couldn't even find his father's grave. Returning to his appreticeship, he found the paper foreman had changed and he was fired. He had saved $12, and was 14 years old, so he decided to catch a riverboat back to St. Louis. He explained his plight to the captain, who let him ride for free, but on the way, his sleeping companion, a drunken Indian, stole his $12, leaving young Kamm with exactly 10 cents in his pocket.

He managed to get a flunky job on the riverboat and joined the steamboat life. Soon he managed to work into an apprenticeship to the ship's engineer, and then he rose to chief engineer on a river packet, *The Hannibal,* the last one built.

Tiring of life on the rivers at age 28 years, he decided in 1849 to come to the West Coast, so he bought a cow and a pony and started across the plains. By then he had stomach trouble, so he brought the cow because milk was about the only food that agreed with him. He joined a wagon train, and took the precaution of paying $100 so he could ride on a wagon if he or his pony gave out enroute. The trip took six months, and Kamm ended up in Sacramento, California where eggs were 50 cents and a pint of milk was 50 cents. He became the engineer of the *Black Hawk,* but the boat burned shortly thereafter.

IN 1850, Kamm came to Portland as the engineer hired to refit the *Lot Whitcomb* with engines. He built the *Jennie Clark,* the first sternwheeler to ply Northwest rivers, and owned half interest in her for his labors.

Then he helped build the *Carrie Ladd,* the fastest boat of her time, and was able to obtain half interest in her, also.

About this time, Kamm and the other persons who had interests in the two boats organized the Union Transportation Company which later became the Oregon Steam Navigation Company. Their interest continued to prosper and grow as the area grew and almost everything had to be moved by water. Ultimately, almost all steamboating on the Columbia River was practically entirely in the hands of the OSN Co., and Kamm, with the largest interest in the company, was president.

Kamm lived to a ripe old age, and until the time of his death kept a tight rein on his companies. ❖

Jacob Kamm

Benson's Founts Foil Saloons

Simon Benson, the man who built Portland's Benson Hotel, was so opposed to liquor that he donated 20 bronze drinking fountains to the city so that workmen would not have to rely on saloons to quench their thirst!

A supporter of prohibition, when the fountains had been installed, Benson sent a trusted agent to discover the effects of the fountains on the liquor business. He was gratified to find that many saloons reported that their sales had dropped 25 to 40 percent.

Scores of other cities followed Portland's example and established public drinking fountains.

Benson was the first chairman of the Oregon Highway Commission and is credited with the change in public sentiment in 1915 that made the paving of Oregon's highways possible. He planned and supervised the construction of the Columbia River highway and personally put up large sums of money for its construction.

Benson's greatest gift to Portland, however, was the Benson Polytechnic School. He contributed $100,000 towards the building and the school board then voted a like amount.

Benson was born in Norway in 1852, and his earliest occupation was farming. After he came to the Northwest, he became involved in the lumber business and he was the first person in the Northwest to successfully conduct all logging with donkey engines. He was also the first lumberman to perfect ocean rafting of logs by developing the cigar-shaped raft.

His Benson Hotel venture lost money at first, but soon became successful, and subsequently became the best-known hotel in Oregon. Benson also built the Columbia Gorge Hotel. ❖

Northwest's first school teacher tried hand at farming, but found climate too wet for him.

First School Teacher

The first school teacher in Oregon arrived at Ft. Vancouver in 1832 from Missouri. His name was John Ball, and he had joined up with Wyeth and walked almost all the way across the country.

Reaching Ft. Vancouver almost penniless, he found Factor John McLoughlin "most kind," and Ball asked what he could do to repay the kindness. McLoughlin replied that guests were not expected to work, but finally it was arranged that Ball would teach school.

His students were the half-Indian children of the gentlemen at Ft. Vancouver who were married to Indian wives. Ball wrote that he had 12 boys as students and that they made "good progress."

He taught them during the winters of 1832 and 1833, then he left to try his hand at farming in the Willamette Valley. The farm was quite successful, but Ball was plagued with fevers and ague from the wet climate. He decided to sell his goods to the fort and to return East. First, however, he decided to visit Ft. George. Here he recorded that a tree had fallen that was 47 feet in circumference.

Obtaining a yawl, he crossed to Chinook Point and walked the three miles to the sea. Of this visit, he wrote:

"So I went alone to look on the broad Pacific with nothing between me and Japan. Standing on the beach of the great Pacific with the waves washing my feet was the happiest hour of my long journey. There I watched till the sun sank in the water. ❖

SOME NORTHWEST HUMOR

Rattlers Rattle Stage

An Eastern scientist wanted a pair of mated rattlesnakes for biology research in the 1870's. He offered to pay $50 for the delivery of such a pair to The Dalles, Oregon.

A man named Woodruff, who owned a stage coach line arranged to get such a pair from someone out on Rock Creek above Goldendale, where there were lots of rattlers. He was to pay $20 for the pair, and planned to make a neat little profit on the deal. The catch was to be made just after the snakes came out of their winter den and were easy to sack.

Finally word was sent that the snakes were ready and Mr. Woodruff came to Goldendale to receive the snakes. From Goldendale, Woodruff and the snakes were to ride the regular stagecoach run to The Dalles.

Besides Woodruff, there were two other passengers on the stage, an old man who ran a flour mill and a lawyer. Woodruff had the snakes in a wooden box which he shoved under the seat so the other passengers couldn't see what was in it.

Unfortunately, the box had a large knot in one end near the bottom. The road was rough and the knot was jarred loose by the jolting and one of the snakes got out. It crawled along the bottom of the stage right under Woodruff's feet.

He saw it and yelled "snakes" and promptly jumped out of the stage head first onto the rocks.

The miller was napping. He woke up and said, "Woodruff's got the dt's. Too much Goldendale whiskey."

By this time the snake had reached his side of the stagecoach. The lawyer saw it, and said,

"Woodruff may have them, but there's a rattlesnake about to get you."

The unperturbed miller looked down and told the snake that if it bit him, it would kill him dead. Then he kicked it back under the seat.

By this time the driver had the team stopped and the passengers jumped out.

Woodruff, rubbing his bruised head, began to worry about how to get the snake back in the box.

The driver said he would put the snake back in for $10. Woodruff said he'd pay $2.50. The driver said the snake could stay in the coach, then, for all he cared. Finally, Woodruff agreed to the $10 fee.

With a forked stick, the driver got the snake headed back into the hole. Then Woodruff backed out, and said he wasn't going to pay anything and the driver turned the snake loose.

This performance was repeated several times, until the other two passengers got sore at Woodruff. Finally, he agreed again that he would pay the $10 price. This time, the snake was all in but the rattles when Woodruff backed out again, saying it was "too easy."

The miller, thoroughly irritated by this time, stepped up and grabbed the snake by the tail

"You give the driver his money right now, or out the snake comes," he said.

Woodruff handed over the $10 and the snake went into the box. The hole was stuffed with a gunny sack and the trip was continued, but Woodruff made $10 less profit on the deal then he had planned on.

Not One Drop More

Mrs. Joe Denny, a highly respected pioneer woman, is credited with this story about early days in the Northwest. She vouched for its authenticity, according to an early editor.

It seems it was the custom for drapery and yard goods stores in the 1850's in the Northwest to keep a barrel of spirits in the back room for their best customers.

A Mr. and Mrs. Flippin were good customers of a store run by a Mr. Smith and Mrs. Flippin bought lots of yardage to make clothing for her rather large family. In fact, the Flippins often spent the day at the store and the proprieter had discovered that the more spirits they consumed, the more purchases they made.

On the day that Mrs. Denny told about, the Flippins had visited the store early in the afternoon, and after they had a few bits of refreshment from the spirit barrel, the proprieter urged them to have more. Mr. Flippin said, "Yes, please," but Mrs. Flippin declined.

"Not a drop more, Mr. Smith, unless it's sweetened," she declared.

The proprieter was quick to oblige and the happy couple then stayed on making their selection of yardage and purchases until it was dusk.

When they finally left the store they had about drunk the spirit barrel dry, but they managed to get on their horse, with Mr. Flippin in front holding the packages and Mrs. Flippin behind him on the horse.

On the way home, the couple had to cross a shallow creek with rather steep banks on both sides, and Mrs. Flippin fell off the horse and into the creek.

Mr. Flippin didn't notice that she was gone and he went

on home. When he arrived, the kids wanted to know 'where is mother?' Mr. Flippin could not offer any explanation. He said she started for home at the same time he did, and on the same horse. Then he went to bed.

The kids set out immediately to try to find mother and they finally found her unharmed, sitting comfortably in the creek and taking little sips of creek water as she mumbled, "Not a drop more, Mr. Smith, though it is sweet." ❖

Two 'Bits' Bought Drink

Almost everyone knows that a quarter is "two bits," and fifty cents is "four bits," but did you ever wonder where those terms came from or how they originated?

An explanation found in an old volume says the expressions "two-bits" and "four-bits" came from liquor dealers in San Francisco during the early days and they were a result of competition.

These were the days during the gold rush when the smallest coin on the West Coast having purchasing power was a quarter. Dimes, nickels and pennies were regarded as souvenirs of the "cheap east" according to the story, and were given to the children to play with. A ten cent piece would buy nothing and most store keepers did not bother to keep them in their tills.

Drinks were 25 cents. Then an enterprising saloon keeper decided to run a bargain and sell two drinks for a quarter. Having no coins to accomplish such a transaction, the saloon then issued iron checks, good for drinks. These were bits of iron, stenciled with the name of the saloon and it was said that they were good for one drink each.

These iron chits were "one-bit" and two of them would buy two drinks. So the quarter came to be called two-bits and fifty cents was four-bits. Other merchants followed suit, and the bits became as common as quarters.

As more immigrants came west and brought more dimes, these became known as "short bits" because one wouldn't buy a drink. Subsequently, a dime and a nickel, or fifteen cents, became a "long bit."

With time, however, the price of drinks fluctuated, the bits disappeared from the market and people forgot about the long and short bits. For some reason, though, the names two-bits stuck to the quarters and four-bits to the fifty cent pieces and we still hear them called that today. ❖

Beirmingham's Rats

An unforgettable character in the early days of Portland was Capt. John Beirmingham, who began visiting the waterfront with his ships when Portland was a small cabin settlement.

For many years, Beirmingham was the chief engineer on an old steamship that began the Portland-San Francisco run in the 1850's. At that time ships tied up at the foot of Everett Street, and the crews had to climb over logs and stumps if they wanted to come ashore.

In his later years, Beirmingham became the U.S. supervising inspector of steam vessels for the First District, which included all navigable waters of the U.S. West of the Rockies.

By this time, he had become affectionately known along the waterfront as "The Ancient Mariner," and it was said that he was very strict about overloading vessels.

However, the story persisted about him that when he was loading his own ships and making the runs, things were different. In those days there was more business than ships to handle it and Beirmingham was noted for piling the freight on the ships as long as they would float.

A friend recalled that Beirmingham's reputation was well known up and down the coast.

"I was sitting on a dock talking to a friend when a 3-legged rat came sneaking around the corner. A second later another rat came along with no tail.

"I observed to my friend that we must be in the accident ward of a rat hospital, but he replied,

"'Oh, no, those are some of Beirmingham's rats.'

"He went on to explain that Beirmingham never likes to leave any freight on the dock so long as there is room in the cabin for a sack of shorts or a box of butter. The result is that he loads his steamers so full that whenever they get in rough water they strain and the seams open and close with the roll of the vessel.

"The rats get careless-like, he said, and step in the seams when they open and of course when they close there is a tail or a leg missing." ❖

Cough Syrup Seal

The official seal of the State of Washington, a bust of the first President, was copied from an advertisement of Dr. Janes' Cure for Coughs and Colds!

George N. Talcott, one of three brothers who were jewelers in Olympia in 1889 and who designed the state seal, made the confession in his later years. He wrote:

"A committee, a short time previous to statehood, appeared before my brother, Charles, at our jewelry store with a design for the proposed state seal, to be completed when the first legislature met in November, 1889.

"The design submitted by the committee was a very complicated sketch, depicting the port of Tacoma, vast wheat fields, and sheep grazing in the valley at the foot of Mt. Rainier.

"My brother told the committee that such a seal would be outmoded with the growth of the state. He picked up an ink bottle from his desk and drew a circle around its base. Next he placed a silver dollar in the circle and drew an inner circle. Now he printed, between the two circles, the words, 'The Seal of the State of Washington, 1889.' He then licked a postage stamp and pasted it in the center, saying, 'That represents the bust of George Washington.'

"His design was immediately accepted.

"In preparing the design for embossing, brother Grant did the lettering and I did the sinking of the die. This cutting to emboss the picture of Washington was done under difficulties. It was my first attempt to cut a die to emboss a person's picture, and it was done under rush orders. To further complicate matters, I had a sick headache. All in all, it was a difficult combination with which to contend. I really believe a much better piece of work would have been turned out under normal conditions. The picture of Washington was copied from an advertisement of Dr. Janes' Cure for Coughs and Colds! ❖

WASHINGTON

Rustler's Prayer Answered

Members of the Methodist Church in Goldendale were holding Sunday Services and a picnic basket dinner in an oak grove a few miles out of town on a nice spring day in 1850.

Long tables were filled with good things to eat and the members were sitting down to the feast when a small dust cloud was noticed on a ridge south of where the services were being held. Shortly thereafter a rider galloped up close to the table. He was recognized as Frank Foss, one of three brothers reputed to be stock rustlers in the area.

Frank's fine horse was covered with white lather. When Frank was invited to dinner, he first rubbed his horse down and cooled him off before giving him food and water. Then he accepted the invitation, sat himself down to the table and ate heartily.

After the meal, he arose and offered the most fervent prayer of the day.

"It skinned all the other prayers by a town block," observed one of the Methodists.

Frank asked the Lord to forgive his sins and save him from impending danger.

Just as he said, "Amen," another, larger dust cloud was seen coming over the hill. Frank did not wait for doxology, but jumped on his horse and galloped swiftly away.

The second dust cloud proved to be the danger Frank had alluded to in his prayer. It was a heavily armed sheriff's posse in pursuit of Frank.

Evidently, his prayer was answered. Frank was not caught but got away and left the country.   ❖

Portland's Webfoot Saloon inadvertantly became target of determined women bent on vanquishing demon rum.

THE WAY IT WAS

Demon Rum Won Round One

The Webfoot Saloon, a respectable early Northwest place as saloons went, inadvertently became the target for warfare in 1874 by the Women's Temperance Prayer League of Portland, a determined bunch of ladies bent on vanquishing the demon rum.

Ultimately, the Crusaders won the battle, but lost the war, or at best delayed the victory another 30 years.

Francis Fuller Victor, a contemporary who was sympathetic to the cause but did not enter the battlefield, wrote about the "War on the Webfoot."

According to the account, drunkenness was "epidemic" in the Northwest in the 1870's. Miss Victor relates that, "The eye-opener set the day in motion, and thereafter many citizens 'op'd their eyes' at regular intervals until they found they could no longer open them at all."

Gentlemen of consequence on occasion nestled down in some convenient gutter, and a jurist of local renown, by applying himself early and often, won the sobriquet "the Whiskey Judge."

In Portland at the time there was a liquor outlet for every 40 persons (counting men, women and children), and these ranged from the famous Oro Fino, to the less respectable Miss Cecilia Levy's Oriflamme.

Preachers firmly denounced liquor from the pulpit, and there were many abstinence pledges circulated. There were also many ladies making the lecture circuit speaking on the evils of drink.

However, no one seemed to be making much headway in the campaign until someone back east got the idea in 1874 for "Praying Down Saloons." Abigail Scott Duniway, outspoken editor of her own paper, called *The New Northwest,* explained the theory in the March 6, 1874 edition of her paper:

"Thousands and tens of thousands of women will blockade sidewalks, interfere with municipal ordinances, sing and pray in the most public places to be seen by men who by this means will be awakened to realize the sense of their political duties."

On March 18, just 12 days later, the Women's Temperance Prayer League was organized and issued a public appeal to saloon keepers urging them to shut up shop.

On March 23 the ladies decided that the war must be carried into the camp of the enemy; they would pray and sing hymns in the saloons! A few of the more conservative ladies withdrew, but the main body was determined.

The next day, twelve women went forth from the Methodist Church on Taylor Street determined to do battle with Demon Rum. They drew an impressive crowd when they visited a saloon at First & Taylor and prayed and sang their songs.

However, two of the ladies, who had been out getting temperance pledges signed, missed the main show, so they decided to make a call on their own. They went into the Webfoot Saloon at First and Morrison.

Walter Mofett, who owned the Webfoot, was a respectable saloon keeper. His wife was a Terwilliger, but Mofett had an intense dislike for female do-gooders. Furthermore, he thought the temperance movement was a tempest in a teakettle, and was hypocritical. Besides, Mofett had a violent temper and a short fuse, and he didn't like ladies in his saloon.

When the two ladies entered the Webfoot, they came face-to-face with a red-faced Mofett, who seized each by the arm and shoved them back out the door.

"Get out," he yelled. "I keep a respectable house and I don't want any street women here."

The startled ladies gasped, and one said, "Why Mr. Mofett, I know you. I prayed with your wife for your safety when you were at sea years ago.

Mofett declared that he didn't want any of their prayers, and they indignantly departed, humiliated and in a huff.

When the two got back to the church, their report electrified the League, cemented the Crusade, and gave it an objective — the downfall of the Webfoot Saloon.

Almost daily, delegations of ladies would visit the Webfoot Saloon, and they were all shuffled off in a hurry. After a few days of this, the ladies decided to change their tactics. On the 31st of March, they marched in a body and arranged themselves in a line in front of the saloon, where they began to pray and sing. A large crowd collected. Then Mofett appeared wearing spectacles and carrying a Bible. He proceeded to read passages in his loudest voice. The ladies sang louder. Mofett shouted. The duel continued for several hours until the ladies withdrew.

The next week the ladies were back again. As soon as they took up their positions in front of the Webfoot Saloon, a huge crowd gathered. In less than three minutes more than a thousand persons showed up. Mofett tried to drown the ladies out with his noise makers, then summoned Police Chief Lappeus. When the chief arrived, Mofett demanded protection of the law and demanded that the Crusaders disperse as they were harassing him. The chief was sympathetic to Mofett's cause, but he kept his sympathies to himself. When he asked the ladies to withdraw, they flatly refused. They replied that theirs was God's cause and their consciences were clear.

The chief then decided there was no alternative but to arrest them, so the ladies trooped down to First Street with him to the jail with the large crowd following.

When news spread of the arrests, fathers, brothers and friends besieged the jail offering bail, but the ladies refused. They were having a fine time and were singing their hymns louder. A judge was hastily sought and dismissed the case when the Leaguers' self-appointed attorney argued that they were not disturbing the peace, but merely exercising their freedom of worship.

The peace that reigned following this episode was short-lived. On April 16, a large delegation of ladies arrived a little after 2 p.m. at the Webfoot. Mofett and his crew set up a hideous din, but this just attracted a larger than ever crowd. Mofett had added an old hand organ and a large Chinese gong to his other noise makers. The ladies had their camp-stools and seemed settled in for the duration. Mofett got purple in the face, after an hour or so, but the ladies sang on.

Finally, one of the bartenders, who had been going back and forth to the bar between gong beatings and was getting pretty drunk, decided to use the hose attached to the fire hydrant at the corner to help disperse the ladies. He turned on the water and the crowd moved back, but the ladies held their ground. Wet to the skin, they did not flinch, but just sang louder.

Discouraged and thoroughly drunk, the bartender began to swear at the ladies. A bystander moved in and hit him squarely between the eyes. The riot had started. Mofett's army, hopelessly outnumbered by the irate crowd, tried to reach the safety of the saloon. Every man who could get through the door followed them in and a wild donnybrook followed. The Webfoot was in shambles. Chairs were thrown, mirrors smashed and bottles demolished.

When the police arrived, the women still were sitting outside singing hymns — they hadn't missed a note. At six o'clock the ladies left. They were back at 10 a.m., and again they brought their stools. The Webfoot was strangely quiet this time. Mofett had gone to bring the police.

Twenty-one women were arrested, but only six were brought to trial. There was a new charge — willfully and unlawfully conducting themselves in a disorderly and violent manner.

This time, Judge Denny ruled that the complaint was proper. On April 20, a jury of six was selected (one saloon keeper and 5 businessmen) and the prisoners appeared before the bar.

The court was packed and the crowd spilled out and packed the street. The trial dragged on for two days, and the jury deliberated a long time before it found the ladies guilty as charged. The judge gave them their choice of a $5 fine or a day in jail.

All six refused to pay a fine and they were put on the third floor of the jail, which immediately assumed a party atmosphere. Visitors and sympathizers came in a steady stream, bringing food, soup and tea. There was lots of hymn singing and praying. By 8:30 p.m. that night, the weary ladies were preparing for bed and settling comfortably down when the chief of police appeared and in peremptory tones ordered the ladies to leave the jail. The women protested. Their friends all had left and they preferred to stay.

"I'm boss here," the chief declared, "You leave."

The ladies got to the street where a large crowd of men was gathered, then fled back to the jail. Finally an escort was found to see them home. Their appearance touched off a demonstration.

The arrest and imprisonment of the Crusaders made them martyrs and gave their cause new strength. Every day they marched in platoons about town. They seemed to be gaining new support for their temperance candidates in the coming election. The feeling was growing that anyone who voted against the temperance candidates was a supporter of sin, un-American and a foe of home and mother.

Then *The Voters Book of Remembrance* under the name of the League, appeared. No one is sure where it came from, but it was rich in four-letter words, blunt language and unseemly clinical descriptions. Overnight, the Crusaders' bright mantle of respectability was destroyed. Preachers retreated from the cause. The temperance candidates were defeated, the ladies retreated.

Saloon keepers decided that prohibition was a pipe-dream, but later the League was resurrected as the Women's Christian Temperance Union and the crusade started all over again. However, it was over 30 years before the crusaders really tasted victory, when prohibition was enacted. ❖

Mayor Axed; Editor Jailed

When the angry president of the Rogue Valley Railroad Company threw an axe at Medford's Mayor and barely missed killing him, the incident set off a series of events that resulted in exposure of corrupt politicians in Jackson County and an editor being thrown in jail.

Even more far reaching, the axe incident led to a 1908 landmark decision in Oregon involving the right of free speech and freedom of the press when the Oregon Supreme Court established that the truth is not libel.

The railroad man was W. S. Barnum, president of a five-and-a-half mile long railroad connecting Medford with Jacksonville. Commissioner Oswald West (later governor) and Medford Mayor Reddy went to visit Barnum following complaints by passengers about deficiencies on his railroad. During the visit, Barnum became enraged and called the mayor all kinds of names. An argument ensued and finally Barnum picked up an axe and struck at the Mayor. At this point, the major and West hastily fled with Barnum in pursuit.

When Barnum saw he was being outpaced, he hurled the axe at the mayor, barely missing his head.

Barnum was brought before the Grand Jury in Medford and charged with assault, but the Prosecuting Attorney and most of the jury were good friends of his and they found the charge "not true."

Crusading editor, George Putnam, of the Medford Tribune, who had been a witness at the attack, was incensed at the decision and wrote a caustic article in his paper. It read:

> A proceeding calculated not only to bring into popular contempt local administration of justice and punishment of crime,

but to force every man to take into his own hands the protection denied under legal process, has just been enacted in Jacksonville by the Grand Jury and Deputy District Attorney Clarence L. Reames. These officers, sworn to enforce the law, have practically justified one man attempting to kill another with an axe.

Then the editor named the jurors, and continued:

It took them just fifteen minutes to indict a friendless horse-thief, a poor old woman, and a penniless forger. They spent three days on the Barnum case and then justified the murderous assault.

The Prosecutor is a relentless prosecutor when a man drops a nickel in the slot machine or takes a drink on Sunday, or a poor fallen creature is caught sinning. Such heinous offenses must be punished; they are dangerous at once to life and limb. But any man can try to brain a man with an axe and secure immunity from the blind-folded representatives of justice.

Following publication of the scathing article, the prosecutor and the jury proceeded to "get even" by indicting Putnam for libel. They waited until the editor was on his way to Portland by train to spend Christmas with his mother, then had him hauled out of his pullman berth at Roseburg and thrown into jail where he was held incommunicado all night and until the following afternoon. The jail was dark, damp, and vermin-infested, he later said.

The editor's trial was labeled a farce, with conviction obvioous from the beginning. When he was found guilty, after not being allowed to present any facts or witnesses about the assault or the truth of his accusations, he announced he would appeal.

At this point, many irate citizens and all the newspapers of Oregon, and some in California and other states, joined the fight. They pointed out that the verdict violated Oregon's statute which said "the truth may be given as evidence and if it appears that the matter charged as libelous is true and was published with good motives and justifiable ends, the defendent must be found not guilty.

"Putnam's guilty verdict said that no matter to what

depths of villainy or corruption an official or judicial body might sink, to publish the facts of its rottenness, even though true, is a crime," declared the *Oregon City Courier.*

The *Eugene Guard* said, "This proceeding was as flagrant an outrage as was ever perpretrated in the state of Oregon."

Governor George E. Chamberlain received so many telegrams and letters that he offered to pardon Putman. Putman declined the pardon and waited for the Supreme Court to act.

After more than a year, the Oregon Supreme Court reversed the decision of the lower court and ordered Jackson County to pay all court costs for Putman.

The new decision brought widespread expressions of approval. The *Oregonian* proclaimed that "every act of every official must be open to investigation and comment as long as nothing but the truth is published about him."

The *Oregon Journal* said, "The right of free speech was vindicated at Salem yesterday."

At the next election, in 1908, every man supported by Putman's paper, the *Medford Tribune,* was elected, sweeping the old political ring out of office. The headlines said Putman had broken the "Courthouse ring led by Sheriff Jackson."

Another result of the affair was the cleaning of the Jackson County jail after the editor's article describing the filth, the rat infestation and the disease-breeding conditions there.

Putman's continued efforts to improve conditions in Jackson County, however, met with physical as well as verbal opposition. He was physically assaulted on two occasions, once by a deputy sheriff and once by a member of the Medford City Council. After these two beatings, and many more threats, Putman obtained a permit to carry a revolver and bought one. Then he announced in his paper that the "open season on editors" was over."

Ready for plunge in ocean, all of these ladies have on their bathing suits, except woman at left with hat and two little girls, right. Vacation at beach became popular in Northwest in late 1800's

Washington Grows Up

Blacksmiths were pounding their anvils, men were firing their revolvers, and the saloon doors were swinging wildly on November 11, 1889, in many towns throughout the Washington Territory.

President Benjamin Harrison had just issued the Proclamation of Statehood for Washington, and everyone was celebrating.

Oregon had become a state 30 years earlier, in 1859. There were those in the Washington Territory who dreamed of having their star in the U.S. Flag much earlier, but there had been no real response on the part of the inhabitants of the large area that extended from the Pacific Ocean. At first, it included all the area to the boundaries of Utah and the north line of Nevada. Subsequent creation of the Montana Territory in 1864 and the Idaho Territory in 1863 shrunk these boundaries; but there was still a narrow strip called the Idaho Panhandle that was in question as to where it belonged.

The Territorial Legislature submitted the question of statehood to the voters in 1869, 1871 and 1873, but the measure met with indifference. Population was scattered, means of transportation and communication were limited, and the hard work of making new homes and coaxing out a living absorbed the interest and strength of the population.

However, in 1876, when the population had increased to about 40,000, the people finally authorized the election of delegates to a Constitutional Convention for the purpose of drawing up a state constitution. The convention sat for 40 days and most of the debates and controversy centered around prohibition of liquor and suffrage. Finally, these questions were dealt with in separate articles, because of fear that their inclusion in the constitution might endanger its adoption by the voters of the Territory at the coming election.

When the voters did vote at the fall election, they favored the adoption of the constitution but turned down both woman' suffrage and prohibition.

Next came the problem of interesting Congress in approving statehood for Washington. Bills introduced for statehood were rejected for various reasons. Politicians charged that the real reasons were political — "fear as to the political bias of the two U.S. Senators who might be accredited as state representatives, or fear as to how Washington citizens might vote in the next presidential election."

In 1886, the bill for annexation was passed by both houses but was vetoed by President Grover Cleveland (by a pocket veto).

Finally, when the fall of 1888 presidential election was over, bills relating to the admission of Dakota, Washington, and Montana were again introduced. The population had grown to 239,000 in Washington, and the state was demanding admission. Reluctantly, and only after much debate, a conference committee of both houses agreed to the admission of North Dakota, Montana, and Washington by Proclamation of the President. President Cleveland signed the enabling act on Washington's Birthday, February 22, 1889.

Another state Constitution Convention had to be held as prescribed by Congress. It met on the 4th of July, and one of the most controversial questions at this session was whether the name of God should have a place in the phraseology of the preamble to the Constitution. Agreement was reached in the statement, "We, the people of the State of Washington, grateful to the Supreme Ruler of the Universe for our liberties, do ordain this Constitution."

Again, the question of woman's suffrage was a hot one, but was not enacted. In 1883-84, the Territorial Legislature had passed an act conferring on women the right to vote in all elections. Women had the vote for two years, but then the courts had pronounced the legislative act unconstitutional.

Not until 1910 did the women of Washington get the right to vote!

Finally, with the constitution approved by the voters, President Harrison issued the Proclamation of Statehood for Washington on November 11, 1889, and touched off the state-wide celebration.

The president did not use a gold pen in signing as is customary on such occasions, but used a quill pen fashioned from a feather taken from the wing of an American Eagle.

"Tenting" at ocean beaches was popular early day vacation in Northwest and families brought everything along, including stove and sometimes kitchen sink, to make their stay comfortable. Everyone came, including grandma and all dressed "properly" for the outing — right down to suits and vests for the men. (Note this family has stove, chairs, table and decorated tent.

Esperanto Fades

What happened to Esperanto, the international language, hailed as "the coming thing" by educators in the early 1900's?

In 1912, when the International Esperanto Convention was held in Portland, it was estimated that 4 million people had learned to speak Esperanto, or were Esperantists." Seventy-eight magazines or journals were devoted entirely to Esperanto. (One of these, *La Simbolo,* was published in Tacoma, Washington.) The same year, a Portland Community Club booklet, with the title which translated, "Oregon, Land of Promise," was published in Esperanto.

Esperanto, said to be an easy language that could be readily learned by anyone and could become an international tongue for all peoples to communicate, was created by Dr. L. L. Zamenhof, a Polish oculist, who was born in Russia in 1859. Because there were four languages spoken in his native town of Bielostoh, Zamenhof was very aware of the need for a common language.

He published his first Esperanto grammar in 1889. (He spoke 22 languages.) The theory of Esperanto was that it had many words in common to all langauges: "telefono, arto, muziko, teatro and telegrafo" were a few such words. It also had a large number of other words belonging to two or three languages: "blua, tempo, granda and inko," to name a few.

Esperanto was far superior to "Volspuk" invented earlier by Abbe Schleyer, because this language, which had short success, was too artificial and did not pay enough attention to already existing languages, said the exponents of Esperanto.

During the first 15 years after Esperanto was introduced, its progress was slow, but steady. In 1904, there were said to be 100,000 Esperantists.

These enthusiastic promoters of the new language declared that it would be "a tremendous stride ahead when all people of each country have acquired in addition to their native tongues, a practical and easy international language which will give them access to the whole world."

In the Northwest, many prominent educators and prominent citizens took up the cause of Esperanto. Mr. and Mrs. J. C. Cooper of McMinnville were two of the most enthusiastic and it was through their efforts that the international Esperanto convention was brought to Portland.

At this convention it was predicted that Esperanto would soon be a required course in all schools and colleges, and that everyone who studied it would be enthusiastic about the new language because it was "absolutely phonetic, and easy to learn because nouns always ended in 'O,' adjectives in 'A' and adverbs in 'E.'"

Today, Esperanto is listed in Webster's dictionary as "an artificial language having a vocabulary based on words in the major European languages." No courses in Esperanto are offered and you don't hear Esperanto spoken on the street corners or anywhere else.

Women Barred From Bars

A newspaper headline in Portland on February 3, 1934 declared, "1500 Women To Be Thrown Out of Portland Jobs!"

A great fuss was raised because of a ruling made by the State Public Welfare Commission, which prohibited women from working in mercantile establishments after 6 p.m.

The women declared that their jobs would be given to young boys at salaries comparable to those of the women discharged. The women were employed in drug stores, dry goods stores, confectionaries, bakeries and similar establishments.

The rules concerning women working in the state's largest city had been adopted in 1919, but the welfare commission had just been given statutory jurisdiction for enforcement to be effective on April 4, 1934.

In addition to the 6 p.m. rule, women working on Sunday was prohibited; the number of hours they could work was limited to 9 per day and 48 hours a week, and the minimum wage was set at 30 cents per hour.

Because the evening deadline for women workers was 8:30 p.m. in other places in the state, the 6 p.m. Portland ruling was protested by women's organizations and the organization of food stores. These groups and irritated women who said their jobs were in jeopardy created such a furor that the new ruling was ended on March 7, 1934, a little over a month before it was to go into effect. The commission edged out of the situation by saying they were suspending the order "for the period of the present economic emergency."

At the time of the ruling there were 8,000 unemployed women in Multnomah County. When the 6 p.m. ruling was taken to court later it was held to be discriminatory. During the court hearings, a Mrs. Alexander Thompson, who said the ruling was sex and class discrimination, charged that the welfare commission was doing nothing about young women employed in establishments where beer was sold!

In answer to this charge, the Chairman of the Commission declared that it was unlawful for women to be employed where intoxicating liquor was sold. ❖

GETTING THERE

Farmers Help Build Railroad

Charges that Portland businessmen were trying to sabotage the Willamette Valley and Coast Railroad Company in the 1880's to prevent Newport from becoming "the San Francisco of the Northwest" were made publicly.

There were reports of newly completed tunnels being set on fire, and bridges burned, but these were doggedly rebuilt and it wasn't until the Portland interests reportedly bought up all the land around Yaquina Bay so that docks couldn't be built that hopes of the Corvallis to Newport railroad promoters finally were dashed. Even then, the railroad was completed and it carried freight and passengers for a number of years.

Following the building of a wagon road from Corvallis to Yaquina Bay in the mid-1800's, the citizens of Corvallis became optimistic about the building of a railroad along the same route. With such a road, Corvallis could be the hub of traffic both north and south, and east and west.

The project was incorporated as the Willamette Valley and Coast Railroad Company, and the people went to the Legislature and asked for a franchise and state aid. No funds were forthcoming, but a contract was drawn between the state and the county stipulating that the franchise be granted and that the railroad would carry men and munitions for the government if called upon.

So great was enthusiasm for the project, that farmers and wagons were enlisted as volunteers. The women came along and cooked and fed the workers. Finally, the first 10 miles of the narrow gauge railroad leading from Corvallis towards Newport was completed, but then the rains came and the farmers went home.

About the same time, a Col. Egerton Hogg visited Corvallis and the coast and saw the possibilities of Yaquina Bay. The Colonel had banker friends and even grander ideas, and he took over.

The railroad would be standard gauge instead of narrow gauge and it would extend from Yaquina Bay to Boise City, Idaho, to connect with the Union Pacific and become the transcontinental route. Yaquina Bay would indeed be the San Francisco of Oregon.

In 1889, the Oregon Pacific Railroad was incorporated by Hogg, Wallis Nash, Sol King and others, with Hogg as president.

One of the first acts of the new company, which absorbed the original railroad enterprise, was to purchase an engine. It was a small, second-hand, diamond stacker named "Corvallis." It arrived by steamer, was floated by barge to Corvallis and was put in a shed because as yet there were no rails.

Indeed, the rails were a problem. Yaquina Bay was not deep enough to ship them in by larger steamer, but the problem was solved by having them carried by the 500 Chinese hired to do the job.

About this time, the little engine, Corvallis, was taken out of its shed and skidded onto a river boat and sent back to Portland, where it was loaded onto a steamship and shipped to Newport, where it went into another shed to await completion of the roadway.

The last spike on the Corvallis-Yaquina Railroad was to be driven on the second week in December, the day the terrible snow of December 1884 began. Twenty-four inches of snow fell, followed by 12 hours of mixed snow and rain, which touched off floods in the Coast Range. Following the flooding, everything froze solid, making all movement of goods impossible.

Supplies were cut off to the train crews still in the mountains — 2,500 men were spread over 70 miles in camps along the track and not even a trail was open. The situation was getting desperate because they only had enough supplies for one week and these were exhausted.

Col. Hogg rose to the occasion, and shouldering a back-pack, he organized and led a relief party with sleds to get food to the stranded men. Soon the tracks were repaired and on December 31, 1884, the last spike was finally driven on the Corvallis-Newport road.

Following this, attention was turned to completing the link of railroad between Corvallis and Boise. Hogg summoned New York financiers and contracts were let for construction to the summit of the Cascades in 1887.

However, the railroad was only built to Boulder Creek, 20 miles short of the summit, before the company finally went into receivership in 1890. At the foreclosure sale, the company was sold for $100,000 in 1894. The $15 million in bonds that had been put up by local people and investors were worthless. Attempts to reorganize the company failed because of dissension among the bondholders and the financiers. ❖

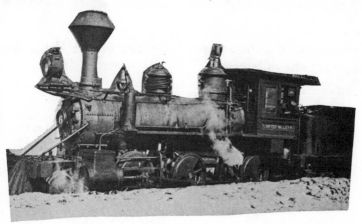

"Clamshell" Railroad stopped to watch lifeboat drills, and anything else of interest.

Railroad Ran With Tide

One of the most colorful narrow guage railroads in the Northwest ran from Ilwaco to Long Beach and Nahcotta, Washington. It was variously called the "Delay, Linger and Wait Railroad," the "Irregular, Rambling and Never-Get-There Railroad," and the "Clamshell Line."

Not only did the train run on an irregular schedule, its service depended on the tide because steamboats could reach the Ilwaco dock only at mid-flood to make connections with the railroad. So, each day for 6 days, departures moved backward 50 minutes, then shifted an entire 6 hours forward.

In addition, the train stopped on the slightest excuse —to pick up passengers along the track, to shovel drifted sand from the curves along the track, or to stop to shoot a bear seen in a nearby field.

Hauling the lifeboat and its crew from Klipsan to anywhere along the beach where a ship was in trouble was a specialty of the train crew. If there was a shipwreck, the train also made a special stop so passengers could take a look.

A weekly attraction in the summertime was also stopping at Klipsan, so passengers could watch the lifeboat drills.

Since the first locomotive on the run was a woodburner, residents cut fuel and stacked it along the track for $2 a cord. The train also made periodic stops to pick up the wood.

Corvallis-Newport Trip Popular

In its hey-day the Corvallis-Newport railroad trip was a popular one. On Sundays, 6 or 7 cars were carried by each section and two sections usually made the run. Most of the travelers were Portlanders on their way to the beach.

The railroad stopped taking passengers in the 1920's, but continued to carry the mail until the 1930's.

During the years when it was running there were some memorable incidents. For a time, a landslide blocked the tracks at the summit of the Coast Range. Fortunately, one section of the two trains was on each side of the slide. It took a long time to get the tracks cleared and, in the meantime, service continued, although not quite as usual. Passengers were taken to one side of the slide. Then they got off the train and walked around the slide and boarded the other train on the other side to continue their journey.

In the 1920's, the great caterpillar invasion of Oregon occurred and, because the caterpillers were ankle deep on the tracks, the train could not get traction. Passengers got off and tried to wipe off the tracks with gunny sacks. (A similar invasion occurred in 1946, but not nearly as bad.)

During the 1920 caterpiller invasion, Oregon Agriculture College (now Oregon State University) was called upon to help, so they imported a fly that got rid of the caterpillers.

Lincoln County lost economically when the excursion trains stopped running.   ❖

OVERLAND MAIL ROUTE
TO OREGON.

Through in Six Days to Portland!!

CONNECTING WITH THE DAILY STAGES

To all the Interior Mining Towns in Northern California and Southern Oregon. Ticketed through from Sacramento, through Marysville, over the Railroad to Oroville, connecting there with the

OREGON LINE OF STAGE COACHES!

To Chico, Tehama, Red Bluff, Shasta, Trinity Centre, Yreka, and in Oregon—Jacksonville, Canyonville, Roseburg, Winchester, Oakland, Eugene City, Corvallis, Albany, Salem, Oregon City, to Portland.

TRAVELERS AVOID RISK of OCEAN TRAVEL

Pass through the HEART OF OREGON—the Valleys of Rogue River, Umpqua and Willamette.

This portion of the Pacific Slope embraces the most BEAUTIFUL and attractive, as well as some of the most BOLD, GRAND and PICTURESQUE SCENERY on the Continent. The highest snow-capped mountains (Mt. HOOD, Mt. SHASTA and others.) deepest ravines and most beautiful valleys

Stages stop over one night at Yreka and Jacksonville, for passengers to rest. Passengers will be permitted to lay over at any point, and resume their seats at pleasure, any time within one month.

FARE THROUGH, FIFTY DOLLARS.

Ticket Office at Sacramento, near the Steamboat Landing.

H. W. CORBETT & Co.,
Proprietors Oregon Stage Line.

July 20 1865

— Courtesy Oregon State Parks & Recreation Division

" SIX DAYS TO PORTLAND"

Baker's Strap Iron Railroad

A physician and surgeon who disliked the practice of medicine built "Baker's Strap Iron Railroad," a marvel of its time to residents of Oregon and Washington.

Dorsey S. Baker graduated from Philadelphia Medical College, crossed the plains to Oregon in 1848, and 1850 found him running a hardware business in Portland, Oregon. He built a flour mill at Oakland, Oregon and boasted that he had brought the first pair of mill-stones into the state. In 1861 he moved to Walla Walla, Washington, and became a partner in a general mercantile business.

The business flourished and in 1862, Baker and his partners branched out into the steamboat business, operating on the Columbia and Snake Rivers. Baker built the tramway at the Cascades of the Columbia, a mule-powered device for transporting merchandise around the rapids.

After selling the tramway to the Oregn Steam Navigation Company, Baker looked around for new worlds to conquer and decided to build a narrow-gauge steam railroad from the Columbia River at Wallula to Walla Walla.

Such a railroad was an ambitious undertaking for its time. Baker's own money represented a large part of the investment. The railroad ties and timbers had to come from the headwaters of the Yakima River. To get them he established his own lumber camp and then had to wait for two years for enough water to float the timbers out.

The first 10 miles of the proposed 30-mile railroad was built on 6 inch by 6 inch stringers laid on cross ties. Baker thought his wooden rails would last for several years, but when they wore out quickly, he bought 10 miles of strap iron to surface the stringers and his road became known as

Baker's Strap Iron Railroad. When the straps also failed, he bought 20 miles of steel rails in Wales and brought them around the Horn in a clipper ship coming to the Columbia River to take on a load of Northwest wheat.

From Portland, the rails had to be handled seven times before they reached Baker...loading and unloading ship twice at the Cascades; twice at The Dalles and once at Wallula. The freight bill was considerable.

Baker ran out of money when his railroad reached Whitman Station, and he began hauling wheat from there to the Columbia River. He wouldn't borrow, and said the terminus would remain at Whitman until the road produced enough revenue to continue it to Walla Walla.

This announcement got the people in Walla Walla very excited because they thought Whitman Station would develop into a rival town, so they raised $25,000 to help complete the line.

When voters rejected a proposal by Baker that Walla Walla County Commissioners guarantee the interest on a proposed bond issue to be sold to private investors, in return for which the commissioners could fix the freight rate, as long as it was not less than $3.00 a ton, Baker became incensed and said he would build the line himself and fix his own rates.

When he finished the railroad, he set the rates at $5.00 a ton from Walla Walla to the Columbia River. As a result, his line paid unheard of dividends, and there was never a mortgage, lien or any debt against it.

In 1877, Baker sold six-sevenths of the stock of his road to the Oregon Steam Navigation Company, but he remained on as President. He then built a branch line from Whitman Station to the Blue Mountains in Umatilla County.

Later when the road was sold to Henry Villard, the track of the Walla Walla to Columbia River was changed to standard gauge, but the Umatilla branch remained narrow gauge.

Baker's railroad was strictly a daylight operation, it never ran at night. Its first passenger car was a converted box car with seats built along the sides.

Baker's Strap Iron Railroad remained a subject for wonder and conversation for many years.　　　-:-

Collie Part of Train Crew

In 1875, a collie dog was officially part of the train crew on the Walla Walla and Columbia River Rail Line which had a regular run between Walla Walla, Washington, and Wallula, a distance of 30 miles.

The dog was specially trained, and was called upon on almost every run between the two points to do his part to keep the train operational.

The Walla Walla and Columbia River Rail Line was built by a Dr. Dorsey Syng Baker, and was built "on a shoestring." Lacking financial backing, Baker decided to use four by six timbers for rails, instead of conventional steel rails. He attached strips of metal to the inside of the timbers to keep the inside edges from wearing.

But the idea seemed to work, and the little teakettle-like engines successfully hauled the grain grown in the Walla Walla hills to Walula where it was transferred for shipping.

However, top speed for the train was aboout two miles per hour and stray cattle on the tracks were frequently a problem to the train's progress.

It was because of the cattle that the collie was trained to ride the train. He sat in the engine until the cattle were sighted on the track ahead, then the alert pooch leaped off, sped ahead of the train and chased the animals out of the way.

People laughed at Dr. Baker's railroad which he started building in 1872, and which took him three years to complete. He operated it for three years after it was c ompleted, and sold it in 1878 to the Oregon Railray and Navigation Company for $1 million.

After he sold the railroad, Dr. Baker and a partner named John Boyer started a bank in Walla Walla. It, too, was a successful operation, and became one of the oldest banks in Washington state.

When the financial crash of 1929 came, one of Baker's sons was operating the bank. Bank after bank across the country closed as the crisis worsened, and one day young Baker received a telegram from the President of Wells Fargo Bank in San Francisco, one of the country's most solid financial institutions. It read,

"Do you need resources? Let me know if I can help you."

The son, replying with the same spirit that had marked his father, wired back,

"Thank you, no. We are solvent, and open for business as usual. Let me know if I can help you."

Horse Cars Too Dirty

Portland's horse-drawn railroad car service came to an end in 1891, when the horses were replaced by electric cars. The companies running the prosperous horsecars were reluctant to make the change, but it was ordered by the city because of complaints about dirty streets.

When the two rival companies, the Willamette Bridge Railroad Company, operating on the Eastside, and the Metropolitan Company on the Westside did decide to convert, there was a great race to see which company would get their tracks down first. The Metropolitan was putting in a track on 2nd street and all the West Side wanted their line to win in the race to the Morrison Bridge. The Eastside company won with a margin of two hours.

Willamette Bridge RR Co. had 4 horse cars in service. Three ran over the Morrison Street Bridge and one ran up Holladay Avenue. The Morrison Street bridge was a toll bridge at that time and it cost five cents to cross whether you walked or whether you rode. "This made the railroad company a paying proposition from the start," one of the conductors recalled. At that time conductors were paid $2.15 a day, for working from 6 a.m. to 10 p.m. each day. Later their pay was raised to $2.25 a day when the cars ran an extra hour, from 6 a.m. to 11 p.m. ❖

Proud conductors on Portland's first electric cars
worked 16 hour shifts for $2.15 per day. Price to ride
across Willamette River bridge was five cents, but rail
service was financial success because it also cost
five cents to walk across bridge.

Soap Only Clue

In 1906 train robbers held up the Oregon rail & Navigation train at Fairview and the only clue they left was a bar of soap.

The train was robbed at 4 p.m. and the robbers escaped with a rather large gold shipment after they blew open a box car.

Three men were involved, according to the train crew, but they could not give an adequate description of them. However, L.H. Huggins, who ran a grocery store in Hood River, said three men came into his store earlier that same day and purchased a cake of soap and a box of matches.

The storekeeper became suspicious, he said, when the men weren't particular about the kind of soap they bought. He sold them a common laundry variety.

Huggins said the men were rough looking characters, and he believed they used the soap to make "dupe" to explode the nitroglycerine used to blow open the express car door.

According to early records, the train robbers were never apprehended and prosecuted, although several suspects were arrested during the ensuing investigation.

Queen of sternwheelers in the Pacific Northwest around the turn of the century was the *Bailey Gatzert,* shown here as she unloaded passengers at a Columbia River landing.

Bailey Gatzert Was Queen

A ride on the elegant and colorful sternwheeler, the *Bailey Gatzert,* often was an exciting trip for early Northwest residents.

The pride of both Puget Sound and the Columbia River, the *Bailey Gatzert* was sleek and fast and her captains and her owners always were ready to race anything else afloat, and they often did!

With her chime whistle blowing, her paddle-wheel churning the water, and the passengers cheering, the - *Bailey Gatzert* was the sentimental favorite, but she didn't always win.

Launchedat Ballard, Washington, in 1890, the *Bailey Gatzert* was without doubt the finest vessel that had yet been launched on Puget Sound. She was named for Seattle's mayor, an outstanding pioneer.

John Leary, president of Seattle Steam and Navigation Company, owners of the *Bailey Gatzert,* proudly announced on launching day that the *Gatzert,* with her 1800 horsepower poppet valve engine, could "easily outrun anything on the Sound."

Placed on the Seattle to Tacoma run, the *Gatzert* soon had occasion to test her abilities. The *Greyhound,* a long, sleek sidewheeler, won the first two heats as the vessels raced.

Something had to be done, the humiliated Leary decided, so cords of the pitchiest slabwood to be found were loaded aboard the *Gatzert,* and the captain was instructed to race the *Greyhound* anytime, anywhere to snatch those victories away from Seattle and Tacoma papers noted that interest in steamboat racing was reaching a new high since the *Gatzert* was added to the Puget

Sound fleet.

Then one March day, as the two vessels were crossing Elliott Bay, the *Gatzert* sounded her passing signal tauntingly as she slowly inched ahead of the *Greyhound*. The lead was gradually widened as the ships churned down Commencement Bay and Captain Hatch held down his whistle rope in a steady blast as the *Gatzert* led her rival by three lengths.

About a month later, owners of *The T. J. Potter,* another sidewheeler, challenged the *Gatzert*. This time the *Gatzert* won easily, and made a lot of persons who had bet large sums on her very happy.

Several times a rematch would be announced, but then one or both ships would be chartered, and disappointed passengers and observers would have to wait for another day.

That day finally arrived and the "showdown" race was on. At Tacoma, both ships were loaded to capacity as they headed to Seattle. Blasts from their whistles alerted Tacomans and they lined the bank of the sound to watch the fun as the ships left the harbor.

In the engine room of the *Gatzert,* pitchy cordwood was piled into her fireboxes as the ships sped towards Seattle. Her pressure gauges rose higher and higher. The paddlewheel whipped up mountains of foam as the *Gatzert* reached maximum speed of 20 revolutions per minute. The boats were evenly matched because they were running neck and neck when suddenly the *Gatzert* blew her nozzle off and up through her stack. The race was over as she skidded to a stop.

One more race was scheduled, but it never came off before the *Potter* was transferred to the Columbia River. She was fast, but she wasn't a rough water ship, so her owners decided she would do better on the river.

John Leary sold the *Gatzert* in 1892 to Capt. H. B. Scott, who ran the White Collar Line on the Columbia River, and shortly afterwards, the *Bailey Gatzert* began the second chapter in her history as queen of the Northwest stern-wheelers.

For two years she ran from Portland to Astoria. Then she was placed as a regular excursion ship from Portland to The Dalles, and for 23 years this graceful "wheeler" carried thousands of happy passengers up and down the Columbia River.

A highlight of the Lewis and Clark Exposition in Portland in 1905 was the excursion ride on the *Bailey Gatzert* to The Dalles. At this time, a special song was written for her, "The Bailey Gatzert Waltz." The trip cost $1.50, including meals.

The racing days of the *Bailey Gatzert* were not over, however, just because she now was a river boat. The *Bailey Gatzert's* new rival was the *Charles R. Spencer,* and every day the steamers left Portland at 8 a.m. and every day was a race. Long, lean and gleaming white, the two vessels competed for the enjoyment of the crew and excursionists to see who could reach The Dalles first. Sizeable side bets were made on the race.

Up the river they churned, their tall stacks billowing smoke, and the paddle wheels churning fountains of water. The one which reached the locks first had a decided advantage, because it took from 45 minutes to an hour to go through the locks.

If a white flag appeared anywhere along the shore, the boat in the lead was required by mutual agreement to stop for pas sengers or freight, thus adding to the excitement of the race and the uncertainty of the finish.

For several years the *Bailey Gatzert* was the official Royal Barge of the Portland Rose Festival, and festooned with gay decorations, it carried the queen and her court up the river to the festivities.

The reverence with which the *Gatzert* was regarded by all who knew her on the Columbia is evident in every historical document. She was the queen and she brought back steamboating and made it a romantic and memorable experience.

The last steamer that master boat-builder John Holland built, he planned the *Bailey Gatzert* to be the finest, most beautiful sternwheeler ever — a monument to his skill. Her interior decoration reflected the pride of the owners and was supervised by a British artist, Harnett. The panels that donned her cabin were the work of a Captain H. Penfield, the first to hold the position of first mate on the *Gatzert*. Money was spent with a lavish hand, making the *Gatzert* a floating palace with an air of grandeur and of glory long passed.

So proud were the crew members of the *Bailey Gatzert* that they often were mistaken for naval officers because of their spotless uniforms and gold braid elegance. Everything on the ship had to be first class.

In 1907, the *Gatzert* was remodeled in Portland and emerged with more tonnage, more length and m ore carrying capacity. But the days of the sternwheelers were fading. Ten years later, the *Gatzert* joined the exodus of the big excursion boats from the Columbia River.

But the *Gatzert* didn't bow out without a final splurge. On June 20, 1917, whe was caught above the Cascades when high water swamped the lifting mechanism in the locks. With more than 100 passengers hanging on for dear life, and her whistles screaming in triumph, she shot through the Cascade rapids and emerged below the Great Chute intact, unscratched and with passengers cheering.

Taken back to Puget Sound in 1917, an older lady with a colorful past, the *Bailey Gatzert* carried passengers between Seattle and Bremerton for several years. She soon became very popular, and her large carrying capacities and easy riding qualities made her a highly successful ferryboat.

But due to the increasing number of automobiles, her new owners decided to give the *Gatzert* a middle-age spread to make her more profitable. She was sponsored out by Todd Shipyards and a vehicle elevator was installed. The *Gatzert* thus became one of the first auto ferries on Puget

Sound.

The *Bailey Gatzert* was retired in 1926, after 36 years of service. She became a floating warehouse for Lake Union Drydocks and was reduced to a barge hauling freight for the Foss Company. She was last seen on Lake Washington, where she probably sank to her final grave...an ignoble end for an elegant vessel that had become a legend in the Northwest. ❖

Mystery Trains Carried Silk

About once a week for almost 20 years heavily guarded mystery trains with white flags flying left Seattle to speed across the continent.

These trains had priority over all other traffic and the tracks were cleared for them as they made their way eastward and many a carload of influential people wondered why their train had been sidetracked to let the flag-bedecked freight train with its oversized engine and oversized boxcars speed by.

These were the famous silk trains that frequently carried over ten million dollars worth of perishable silk to the eastern seaboard from the port of Seattle. They had top priority on the railroad over any other train on the tracks and ran from approximately 1910 to 1930.

Schedules of the silk trains were a closely guarded secret. Insurance costs on the cargo ran as high as $2,000 a day.

The silk was shipped by steamship from Japan and China to the port of Seattle where it was transferred to the train for transport to the textile mills in the east. The transfer of cargo from the ship's hold to the railroad cars was guarded as closely as any shipments of gold.

Once the 28 tons of bailed silk were loaded into each specially designed box car, and the car sealed, a special car holding railroad detectives was attached and the silk train got under way.

All along the route the word was flashed, the tracks were to be cleared — every other train was instructed to yield the right of way. The silk train could cross the continent a full day faster than any other train. Speed was critical as the raw silk was delicate and needed to be processed as soon as possible.

For almost 20 years these trains caught the imagination of people living along the railroads and crowds would gather to watch the silk trains with their white flags flying, even though their schedule was supposed to be secret.

The tight security was attempted because the detectives feared hijackers and always worried when the trains were forced to stop for any reason.

About 1930, the demand for silk declined with the introduction of rayon to the clothing market. As the big textile mills turned to the newer synthetics, the silk trains became a thing of the past, and another page was turned on another era of Pacific Northwest history. Today there are few who remember the speeding silk trains that hurried eastward with their expensive and perishable cargo. ❖

SKULLDUGGERY & CONNIVING

Northwest Hostage Crisis

The Northwest had what may have been the first American hostage crisis 130 years ago, and at the time it caused as much consternation and executive headache as the Iranian hostage crisis of the 1980s.

In 1851, 27 Northwest pioneers set out to "strike it rich" in the new gold fields at Gold Harbor, Queen Charlotte Islands, but instead of obtaining riches at this new "Eldorado of the North," the Americans became hostages and almost lost their lives.

In the summer of 1851, a Captain Rowland sailed into the Northwest with his trim little sloop, the "Georgianna," and learned about the fabulous gold strike at Gold Harbor. Impressed with the gold specimens that he saw and the stories that the ledges were so rich that the gold could be cut from veins with cold-chisels, Rowland advertised for passengers and on November 3, his sloop loaded with 27 persons sailed northward in the storm-tossed coastal waters.

At the time, the islands north of Puget Sound were inhabited by the most treacherous Indians of the entire Northwest territory, the Haidahs.

First, the Georgianna was forced to seek refuge from the stormy seas in Neah Bay at the mouth of the Strait of Juan de Fuca. When the ship finally sailed again, it encountered storm after storm, as well as dense fogs. When a sudden gale threatened to drive the little ship aground, the captain found it necessary to anchor in a small bay off one of the islands. During the night, the storm increased and the Georgianna's anchor dragged and the ship was soon in the breakers.

As the ship began breaking up, a man managed to get a line ashore, but the Indians were waiting on the beach to seize the Americans as each one made it to shore. The unfortunate shipwreck victims were then stripped of their clothing and the remains of the sloop was looted and burned.

The Indians made slaves out of the gold seekers and the ship's crew. They were forced to carry wood and water to the Indian lodges and to perform other hard labor. With barely enough food furnished them to keep them alive, the cold, wet, starved and mistreated men were in desperate circumstances.

After several weeks, one of the men persuaded the Indians to take him by canoe to Ft. Simpson, controlled by the Hudson Bay people. He had convinced the Indians that the hostages could bring them generous rewards if the authorities knew of their plight.

The Hudson Bay people were friendly and sympathetic, but said they were in no position to take action and the Indians became even more hostile. Fortunately, another ship, the Damaris Cove, had set out for Gold Harbor at about the same time as the Georgianna. It reached its destination, and somehow the captain of the Damaris Cove, alarmed when the Georgianna didn't show up, learned of its fate and the plight of the captured American hostages. However, the captain was afraid to go to their rescue because he feared for the safety of his own ship and crew.

Instead, he hurried back to Puget Sound and informed the Collector of U.S. Customs about the plight of the 27 Americans.

The nearest U.S. vessel was at San Francisco, so on his own initiative, the Collector charted the Damaris Cove, fitted her with four cannons and 25 specially picked-up men to supplement the crew, and put aboard a quantity of goods to use for ransom.

On December 9, the armed ship reached the bay where the hostages were being held, and after considerable bargaining, the captain was able to secure the release of the men.

The price for each hostage was five blankets, two shirts, one bolt of muslin and two pounds of tobacco.

The starving Americans had been mistreated slaves of the savage Indians for 54 days.

When the Collector reported the rescue to the U.S. Treasury Department, along with a bill for the costs incurred, he was told that he had acted without authority and that the rescue was unwarranted, so the bills could not be paid.

It was several years later before he was finally reimbursed for the expenses, after much political wrangling and many heated arguments with officials in Washington, D.C. ❖

Hard-working teams of oxen hauled most of logs out of Northwest woods when logging first began here. Good animals were expensive and mostly well cared for, sometimes even provided with leather shoes. Man carrying grease walked behind team and greased skids to help logs move.

Peter French

Why Peter French Was Shot

A manuscript has been called to our attention that sheds light on Peter French and his activities and gives some good reasons why he was shot and why the man who shot him went "scott free." This original manuscript, now in the University of Oregon Library, was written by David Shirk, who was also a cattleman in Eastern Oregon during the terrible depredations of hostile Indians and the range warfare with Peter French.

David Shirk said he was at one time good friends, "cronies, in fact," with Peter French. Their parting of the ways started over a girl — pretty Frances Crow, who was courted by both men and won by Shirk, who married her in April 1877.

Following the marriage, Shirk, who up to that time had spent most of his adult years on rugged cattle drives from Texas to the Northwest, decided to settle down and filed a claim on land on Home Creek in Southern Oregon's Catlow Valley.

Shortly after this, the Bannock Indians went on the warpath, burning farms, killing cattle and horses and killing and scalping any and all whites that they could catch. As many as 2,000 warriors roamed the Steens Mountain and surrounding areas.

Shirk sent his wife to California and stayed on his new farm to protect it. Peter French was temporarily driven from his nearby Diamond Vally ranch and his Chinese cook was killed. But both Shirk and French survived the war.

When the Indians were finally defeated and the war was over in 1878. Shirk found his losses less than he expected (only about 75 head of horses killed) and he settled down.

"We were now beginning to realize that if we were to remain in the livestock business, we must secure title to land and prepare food for our stock during the winter months," Shirk wrote. Until that time the abundant wild bunchgrass and white sage had kept the cattle fat and all the cattlemen had to do was round them up in the spring and fall and brand the calves. At the fall collection, beef were driven to market, usually to Winnemucca for shipment to the markets in San Francisco.

By 1884, there were so many cattle in the area that the land acquisition scramble was on in earnest and every cattleman was making every effort to acquire title to more land by filing on all rights that the law allowed.

From 1878 to 1884, title to land could be acquired by the Homestead Act, by preemption, desert, and timber culture acts. Shirk had managed to secure title to 1240 acres of land which required about 8 years to perfect, provided no contests were instituted.

"But while we were endeavoring to acquire title to this land, the French-Glenn Company and other cattle barons were appropriating land by the tens of thousands of acres, and by every means, foul and fair," Shirk wrote.

"A corps of gun fighters were maintained by French to browbeat and intimidate settlers on the public domain, and small stock owners settling in the country were submitted to such annoyances, threats and despicable acts that they soon gave up and sold out for whatever they could

"By this means, the cattle barons sought to control an empire in what was then the southern end of Grant County and designated the Steen Mountain country," Shirk declared.

Shirk contends that his brother, who had an adjacent farm, and he were "small fry," but said that they held the key to the Catlow Valley range and controlled most of the water there. For this reason, he said, the "Cattle Kings" were determined to freeze the Shirks out.

Peter French began laying a string of 40-acre script land around the west side of the Shirks' land and built a 5-wire fence which would shut the Shirks from their western range. French allegedly closed a long-traveled road that ran through this strip. In addition, Shirk said that French "hired men to contest our holdings and backed them up by telling them that 'if you get into trouble with the Shirks, we will buy you out.'"

Shirk said the culmination came when a man named Isaacs was hired by French "to jump some of our land."

On August 8, 1888, Shirk was confronted by two claim jumpers, Isaacs and another, who were armed and threatened to shoot him. Shirk ordered them off his land, and in the foray, Isaacs was shot and killed by Shirk.

It was brought out in the trial that French had agreed to pay Isaacs $1000 for his claim on the Shirk property, plus all his expenses and would "buy him out in the event he got in trouble with the Shirks."

Shirk surrendered after the shooting and was tried in Canyon City, and it was openly charged that French had succeeded in purchasing a member of the jury to hang the jury if he could not secure a conviction. This the man did.

Before a second trial could be held, Grant County was divided by Legislative Act and Harney County formed from the southern portion. Shirk was retried in the new Harney County Court and acquitted.

According to Shirk, French continued his tactics of harassing the settlers. Meeting one of them in the late part of the 1890's, "French engaged him in a quarrel, ending by striking the man, named Oliver, over the head with a riding whip. Oliver drew his gun and shot French dead.

"A trial was held and resulted in the acquittal of Oliver, the employees of French appearing as the main witnesses. Thus ended the life of Peter French, a man of many admirable qualities of mind and heart, but whose tyrannical and overbearing temper brought about his own ruin. He lived a life of violence and by violence he died," declared David Shirk, writing his memoirs in 1920, at the age of 74. ❖

Ebey Lost His Head

The unfortunate Colonel Isaac N. Ebey, collector of customs living on Whidby Island in Puget Sound, was the wrong man in the wrong place at the wrong time.

The result was that he lost his head to a group of revengeful Haida Indians.

In the mid 1850's it was customary for the Haida Indians from Vancouver Island to bring their families to the Puget Sound country for the summers. The squaws would work in the mills or as domestic help while the braves hunted and fished and generally enjoyed life.

Just prior to the Indians returning to their homeland each fall, the braves would start stealing whatever they could to find to take back north with them.

It was the fall of 1855, and the residents of Fort Gamble were irate because of the robberies by the Haidas who were preparing to depart the area. Finally, the townspeople forced the Indians to gather their belongings and leave the townsite. The Indians were not ready to return to their homes, so they camped across the bay and continued to come into town at night and take whatever they could find that wasn't tied down.

At the time, the warship USS Massachusetts was in the harbor and the people from Fort Gamble asked the captain to confront the Indians and scare them off.

The Massachusetts sailed out into the bay and opened fire on the Indians' camp, killing their "Tyee" or chief. The Indians hastily broke camp and set out in their canoes for home.

Two years later a group of Haida warriors returned to Fort Gamble with the purpose of finding and killing Dr.

George Kellogg who they thought was the white man "Tyee" in retaliation for the death of their chief.

However, in the intervening year, Dr. Kellogg had moved to Whidby Island. The Indians were told that he lived near Admiralty Head so they started out to find him.

Fortunately for Dr. Kellogg, he had gone to Washington, D.C. on business when the Indians arrived at his residence. Frustrated by the chain of events, the Indians decided to locate the most influential man on the Island and kill him for the revenge.

The Indians spent a week on Whidby trying to figure out who to kill. Finally, one afternoon in desperation they saw a distinguished looking white haired man working in his garden. Asking a passerby if that man was famous, the man questioned laughed and was said to reply, "Yep, about as famous as they come around here."

At 11 p.m. that evening, the Indians knocked on Col. Ebey's door and when he stepped out to see who was there they shot him and removed his head, taking it with them.

A search party was hastily organized to try to intercept the Indians before they reached their boats, but it was foggy and the warriors slipped away in the fog.

Two years later, the Hudson Bay Company pressured the Indians into returning Col. Ebey's head, and Judge Swan brought it to the family for proper burial.

Needless to say, the northern Indians were no longer welcome on Whidby Island in the years following this episode. ❖

Pig War Contrived?

Did two army officers, along with Washington's Governor Stevens, try to avert the Civil War in the U.S. by starting a dispute with Great Britain, the idea being that if they could get a rumble going with England, America would forget about its internal struggle and the war that might destroy the country would be averted?

Some historians suggest that this may have been at the bottom of the "Pig War" that occurred in the San Juan Islands and centered around the minor boundary dispute between England and America.

The treaty with England over the disputed boundary of the entire Oregon country was signed in 1845 when the boundary was set at 49 degrees parallel. However, the treaty left in question part of the San Juan Islands in Puget Sound.

James Douglas, British Columbia Governor at Victoria, placed sheep on San Juan Island in 1853. Col. Isaac N. Ebey, U.S. Collector of Customs for the Puget Sound area, found the sheep in 1854 and said they were on American soil. The sheep were subsequently assessed by the U.S., and Douglas refused to pay the taxes, saying the land belonged to England. The Americans then snatched some of the sheep to pay the taxes and diplomatic exchanges followed. Commissions were appointed by both governments in 1856, but evidently with instructions which prevented them from reaching any agreement.

Nothing much happened until an American killed a troublesome pig belonging to a British peace officer. The American frightened off British officers who tried to arrest him by reaching for his gun.

In the excitement that followed, the Americans on the

island asked General Harney for military protection "against the Indians." A company of troops from Bellingham Bay was sent under the command of George E. Pickett, who later led the Confederate charge at Gettysburg. Harney's orders made it plain that not Indians but protection adn resistance to all attempts at interference by the British authorities "by intimidation or force" was the reason for the troops.

In retaliation, the British sent three ships to the island. America's General Pickett said he would fire if the British attempted a landing. He was backed by General Harney, who then dispatched all available troops from Fort Townsend and Fort Bellingham to the Island.

Fortunately, the British did not open fire when the additional troops arrived, but awaited orders from their government. Lt. General Winfield Scott, commander-in-chief of the American Army, was ordered to the scene. He hastily arranged for joint occupancy of the island until things could be settled, and ordered the hot-headed Pickett removed from command.

However, as soon as Scott left, General Harney again placed Pickett in command. Scott, highly irritated at this action, called it to the attention of the War Department as evidence of lack of sympathy with the peace efforts. Harney was at once recalled from the Coast.

At about the same time, the Civil War broke out and the war department had other worries. The San Juan dispute was finally referred to Emperor William I of Germany for arbitration. A decision was given on October 12, 1872, in favor of the United States and in 1873, Washington State created San Juan county to include the disputed island. ❖

No Winner Battle

An 1858 land battle with no winners raged in Salem for 16 years. The outcome was a compromise with both sides probably spending more on the litigation than they ever realized from the property involved.

The long litigation held up Salem city imrovements and one of the landowners in the squabble was dead before the thing was finally settled.

In February 1850, J.B. McClane and another man laid out the township of North Salem on their two land claims. Such town platting was a favorite pastime of early Northwest claim holders — many cities were platted, and some of them materialized, and some didn't.

In the case of the North Salem plat, things looked good. Business was booming because of all the gold brought back from the California gold rush, and Mc Clane's North Salem Flour Mill was prospering.

Three years later, McClane decided to sell his North Salem Mill, along with his property and to move his family back East. He had completed a residence requirement on the land claim of more than 7 years, and having made and filed his final proof of contract, residence and cultivation, according to the laws of the Oregon Donation Law, he thought everything was in order for the final sale.

Then in September of the same year, John D. Boon, who had bought several of McClane's lots, "jumped the claim" on McClane's property, saying that McClane, because of temporary absence of nearly 7 months from the claim in 1849-50 (while McClane was hunting gold in California), the claim had been interrupted because continued residence had not been made and the claim was therefore invalid.

Boon, assuming the title was vitiated and therefore fraudulent, filed notification of occupancy on the land.

The long litigation followed. Boon died in 1854, but the suit went on with his heirs taking up the battle. McClane received his U.S. patent on the land in 1861, and the suit was remanded to the Supreme Court of the United States.

Eight years later, Boon's heirs and McClane closed the case by compromise, leaving both sides with heavy losses from the long legal fight and legal fees. ❖

Officials Chastised

Early settlers in the Washington Territory east of the Cascades saw little need for government, and resisted all attempts to be governed for as long as possible.

The first families to come to this area arrived in the years of 1858 and 1859. It was in 1859 that Oregon was detached from the Territory and became a state. The territorial governor tried to organize counties shortly thereafter, but didn't have much cooperation.

In Klickitat County, a mock election was held in 1860, but no one bothered to take the oath of office. The residents declared there was no need for government.

Again in 1861, there was a government attempt to reorganize Klickitat County. Persons were appointed to fill the vacant offices. In 1865, there were still no county records. Some taxes had been collected, but the county officers divided these among themselves.

The first sheriff appointed himself tax collector then left town with the money he had collected.

Things went on completely unorganized until 1867 when officers were again appointed by the territorial government and were told of their duties. They were told that reports had to be made to Olympia as provided by territorial statutes.

The residents held a conference and then advised the government that the settlers were not compelled to levy and collect taxes for things that officials at Olympia wanted because the matter of establishing Klickitat County had never been submitted to a vote of the people.

Nothing more was heard from Olympia until late in the spring of 1867 when a determined gentleman on horseback arrived. He wore a badge which proclaimed him to be a representative of Uncle Sam.

He had warrants from the territorial district court of Olympia charging all the county officials who had failed to qualify and perform their duties with an offense under the criminal code.

The officials were rounded up and taken overland by Snoqualmie Pass in a horseback cavalcade.

As they neared Olympia, the nervous officials aked the deputy if they were to be put in jail.

The officer replied that there was a jail for criminals in Olympia, and said it would be up to the judge.

Upon their arrival, the U.S. Marshall did not order them locked up. He said he had been instructed to take them to a hotel. The next day, they were taken to court, but instead of being put on trial, they were ushered into the judge's chambers.

Whereupon the judge gave them a thorough lecture on the United States Constitution. Then he pointed to the flag and reminded them of their patriotic duty as good citizens. He said he was sure they were good citizens and that he did not want to impose a fine on them which he knew would have to be paid by serving jail sentences.

After all this, he asked them if they could go home and perform their duties as county officials, provided he continued the case against them indefinitely.

All promptly agreed and went home happily and properly chastised.

Klickitat County had a county government from then on. Livestock brands were registered for the first time in 1868, but there was no jail established for another 20 years.

The Terrible Oregon Boot

A terrible device for restraining prisoners known as the "Oregon Boot," or the "Gardner Shackle," in the early days was developed by a warden at the Oregon State Penitentiary in 1862. Over the years, the invention netted him a nice profit before its use on prisoners was discontinued a few years ago as being too inhuman.

As late as 1960, the Oregon Boot still was being used by some law enforcement agencies for transporting prisoners about the U.S.

The boot consisted of an iron stirrup fitted about the foot of the convict with a 15-pound weight fixed in a locked position about the leg and supported by the stirrup. The device made it almost impossible for a prisoner to run or even to move about.

Early law enforcement authorities said it was not possible to hold prisoners without the Oregon Boot and it was adopted and used throughout this country as well as in other countries. In 1866, Gardner secured a patent on the boot and obtained a restraining order from the court preventing its use without compensation to him.

In 1873, Oregon State Penitentiary Superintendent Watkinds had this to say about the Oregon Boot:

"A great wrong we are compelled to put on the prisoners for want of sufficient walls is the Gardner shackle. There are prisoners who have worn this instrument of torture, known inside the prison as a mankiller, until they are broken down in health and constitution... it is murder of the worst type."

Without question, the lack of jails in Oregon in the early days was the motivation for the boot's development. Until 1845 there was no jail at all. Then a two-story jailhouse was constructed at Oregon City. The first floor of this jail housed the prisoners. There was only an outside stairway to the second floor. Prisoners were let down into the first floor by way of a trap door in the middle of the second story floor. A guard stood at the top of the trapdoor with a club to bash over the head any prisoner who tried to escape.

This Oregon City Jail burned the year after it was built, and for 10 years there was no prison. A case in 1850, when Francis Pressie was tried for manslaughter and sentenced to 7 years, pointed up the need. The judge said that until a jail was prepared. Pressie would have to be kept in the sheriff's house.

The Legislature of 1851 passed a bill authorizing construction of a prison, but nothing was done for two years, so in 1853 they passed another bill. After four years of wrangling a prison was started on two blocks in downtown Portland between Hall and Harrison Streets on Front Avenue.

In the meantime, an old record indicates that keeping prisoners without bars was a problem:

Oregon City, 1853 — "Clatawad, the lone Indian, who has been here for sometime, not liking the untutored simplicity of the accommodations provided him, has left. He was convicted of stealing horses and was sentenced to five years."

Prison labor was used to help build the Portland jail, and evidently the prisoners mostly came and went at will. The record for October 22, 1853 noted that "the robber named Sellers has escaped custody, and the Indian who was convicted of stealing horses has left again."

The Portland Penitentiary was completed in 1857, but nine years later, it was decided that it should be moved to Salem. It seems the Portland institution had been built on two blocks, crossing a street in between. The builder had neglected to obtain title to one of the blocks to the street. The building, which cost $85,000 to construct, was sold for $6,000. The cornerstone for the state penitentiary at Salem was laid in 1871. ❖

Doctor Recruiter

An early day Oregon physician who was a surgeon, soldier of fortune and prospector, dutifully tended the ills of residents along the southern Oregon Coast for two years, 1853-1855, and none of his patients or neighbors suspected that his true purpose here was intrigue and illegal activities.

Dr. Alonzo Hubbard came west from Scituate, Massachusetts, he said, to look for gold, and he settled in the Kelly Hotel, 3½ miles north of the mouth of the Rogue River, and began working a black sand beach at the foot of Hubbard Mound.

Soon people were talking about his skill as a physician and surgeon. His most notable surgery was on an Indian chief from the lower Rogue, known as "Whistling Trigger."

The chief had been injured in the face during a battle and when he healed his mouth was sealed, except for a very small opening. When he tried to speak, the only noise he could make was a whistling sound. Eating also was problem.

Dr. Hubbard became friendly with the Indians and persuaded the chief to let him do surgery on him to repair the damage. When the chief and his squaw arrived at the appointed time for the operation, they both were nervous. At the sight of blood when the operation began, the wife began yelling and shouting and it took both the doctor and his assistant to keep things quiet enough for the operation to proceed.

When the doctor was done, he instructed the chief to keep a green willow stick between his lips until the incision healed.

So successful was the operation and so pleased was the chief when he found that he could again talk and eat normally that he reappeared at the doctor's residence one day with two of his daughters. He had brought one for the doctor and one for the doctor's assistant!

Dr. Hubbard thanked the chief, but told him he already had a wife. The assistant hid out in the woods for a week.

It later was discovered that Dr. Hubbard was a recruting sergeant for William Walker's Raiders in Nicaragua, and that he had enough muskets hidden his premises to arm a whole company.

Walker, who was infamous at the time, was the Tennessee filibusterer who had tried to conquer Lower California and the State of Sonora, Mexico. When this failed, he was arrested for violating the U.S. neutrality laws.

Walker then turned his attention to Nicaragua, which had been independent since 1838, but was still having a dispute over the site for the capital city. When Leon managed to get the capital at Managua in 1855, he engaged Walker to help keep it there. Walker then stepped in and took over complete control of the young nation and declared himself president.

Dr. Hubbard, who was in cahoots with Walker, was sent to the Northwest to recruit reinforcements from among the disillusioned gold miners and the discharged troops from the Indian wars.

Walker later was captured by the government in an attack on central Honduras and was executed. The fate of Dr. Hubbard was unknown. After he hastily left Oregon, he was never heard from again.   ❖

Conspiracy Revealed

The plot to kill President Abraham Lincoln in 1865 was disclosed four days before he was assassinated, but the justice of peace who received the information thought it was unimportant!

This disclosure was made by a Northwest pioneer who came here in 1880. At the time of Lincoln's death, she was 28 years old, a friend of the Lincolns and she attended the trial of the conspirators concerned in Lincoln's assassination.

Fred Lockley of the *Oregon Journal* interviewed 88-year-old Mrs. Wingard in 1925 and wrote her story of the assassination.

Mrs. Wingard said her husband was a lawyer and they were personal friends of the Lincolns and she visited Mrs. Lincoln frequently.

"My husband told me that President Lincoln and his wife were to attend the performance at Ford's Theatre on Friday night, April 14, 1865, and he asked me if I cared to go. I said, 'No, I cannot go as Friday is Good Friday, but I do not mind your going.' "

"He and my nephew, John Bingham, who was my husband's clerk, went and they saw John Wilkes Booth kill President Lincoln.

"On the morning that President Lincoln was assassinated, John Wilkes Booth took a carpenter to Ford's Theater and had him fix a bar on the door to the president's box that overlooked the stage.

"In telling me of the tragedy he had witnessed, my husband said that Booth, after shooting President Lincoln, jumped from the box to the stage and turning to the audience, shouted, *'Sic semper tyrannis.'* He then stumbled off the stage and through the stage entrance to where he had a saddle horse waiting in the alley. The audience was dazed and appalled.

"President Lincoln was carried to a house across the street from the theater, Mrs. Lincoln going with her husband. Booth went to the home of Dr. Mudd, who cut the boot from his injured foot, dressed it an put his leg in splints. Booth continued his flight and took refuge in Garrett's barn near Bowling Green, Virginia, where he was discovered and, after a siege, was shot by Sergeant Boston Corbett.

"My husband's sister had married a brother of John A. Bingham, the special judge advocate who conducted the trial of the conspirators concerned in the assassination of President Lincoln. Because of this relationship we were given tickets admitting us to thetrial. My husband and I were assigned seats about 10 feet from the prisoners, so we had a good opportunity to see and hear everything that went on at the trial.

"It was brought out in the trial by Judge Bingham that the conspirators had plotted to assassinate President Lincoln, Vice President Johnson, Secretary of State William H. Seward, Secretary of War Edwin M. Stanton, and General U.S. Grant, in command of the army. He also brought out the fact that a man named Kennedy was to set fire to a large number of buildings in New York City in the hope of destroying it. Much of the plotting was done by the conspirators in secret meetings in Canada. It was also planned to destroy as much shipping and as many wharves as possible.

"He also brought out the fact that the plot was first hatched in the fall of 1864. It was brought out that the choice of the man to kill the president lay between John Wilkes Booth, Harper, Caldwell, Randall, Harrison and Surratt. It was also shown that Dr. Merritt, who was familiar with the plans, did not countenance the killing of President Lincoln and on April 10, four days before the assassination, he filed information of the proposed plot to kill the president with Judge Davison, a justice of the peace in Canada, who did not attach much importance to the statement.

"It would be too long a story to tell you all the evidence brought out in the trial, so I will make it short by saying that George A. Atzerodt, David E. Herrold and Lewis Payne were executed and their bodies buried in the arsenal at Washington, D.C. Mrs. Mary E. Surratt was also executed. She was buried about a mile outside of Washington and I have often seen her gravestone, which bears an inscription containing her name and the date of her death. Dr. Mudd was sentenced to 10 years in the penitentiary at Dry Tortugas. Lieutenant Colonel Rath was in charge of the execution of the conspirators. It was supposed that the body of Booth was sunk in the Potomac, but Lieutenant Colonel Rath had the body secretly buried in the arsenal at Washington, D.C.

"One of the interesting things at the trial of the conspirators was a letter dropped by Booth, which was found and delivered to Major General Dix and by him turned over to the war department on November 17, 1864, five months before Lincoln was shot. The letter was written by Charles Selby and was as follows:

" 'The time has at last come that we have all so wished for, and upon you everything depends. As it was decided before you left that we were to cast lots, we accordingly did so and you are to be the Charlotte Corday of the nineteenth century. When you remember the fearful, solemn vow that was taken by us, you will feel there is no drawback. Abe must die, and now. You can choose your weapons — the cup, the knife, the bullet. The cup failed us once and might again. Johnson, who will give you this, has been like an enraged demon since the meeting because it has not fallen upon him to rid the world of the monster. . . . Strike for your home; strike for your country; bide your time, but strike sure.'

"President Lincoln was shot at ten minutes past ten o'clock on the night of April 14. At the same time, Lewis Payne entered the sick room of Secretary of State Seward. He stabbed Seward in the throat and face, and wounded Seward's son and two attendants before he broke away and fled. George Atzerodt was interrupted in his attempt to kill Vice President Johnson at the Kirkwood House.

"Generat Grant had taken the evening train from Washington and the man assigned to kill him did not learn of Grant's change of plans in time to take the train with him and kill him."

Mrs. Wingard told Lockley that shortly after Lincoln was killed, her husband was transferred to San Francisco. Then they moved back to Washington, D.C. after a brief assignment in Portland, Oregon. From there théy went to Salt Lake City where they became friends of Brigham Young. Wingard was instrumental in getting two of Young's sons appointments to West Point and Annapolis.

After Wingard's death in 1880, Mrs. Wingard moved to Bingham's Springs in Oregon, one of Oregon's popular mountain resorts of the 1880's. She was manager there for 7 years before she moved to Portland.

"From here I went to Cannon Beach and took up a homestead.

"At that time there were no roads to Cannon Beach. We managed to get along with trails through the woods. Seaside was a small village to which some of the well-to-do families from Portland came down each summer. Long Beach was the popular resort in those days."

Mrs. Wingard lived at Cannon Beach for 37 years before her death in 1925.

New Clues to Treasure

Earl Reeder, 83, a direct descendant of J. E. Reeder, the Sauvie Island pioneer, says he believes the buried gold from the "wrecked beeswax and treasure ship" at Nehalem on the Oregon Coast is still there.

But, Reeder says, it is not on Neahkahnie Mountain where everyone has been looking for it for over 130 years.

Reeder's information is based on the story of the shipwreck and gold burial told to his grandfather Reeder by the Indians. The story persists that the Reeder family had a map to the buried treasure given to the elder by the Indians, but Earl Reeder denies any knowledge of such a map. He is convinced, though, that the search for the treasure has been carried on in the wrong area.

The Reeder story of the burial of the gold coincides closely with other stories that have become legend.

The Indian tale is that long before white men came to stay in the Northwest, several ships appeared off-shore. "Poofs" of smoke rose as the vessels neared each other and then all but one of the ships sailed off. Men from the disabled ship came ashore to make repairs, but before they were finished a storm came up and drove their ship aground. After this happened, they carried a large, heavy chest up the beach, dug a hole and buried it. Finally, they shot and killed one of the men who had done the digging and buried him with the chest. He was a black man.

The Indians, being superstitious of the dead, stayed away from the place and did not disturb the chest.

As early as 1850, white men who heard the story from the Indians began looking for the treasure. They are still looking. Over the years, thousands of holes have been dug on

Neahkahnie Mountain. The mountain has also been the scene of some serious research by historians.

A few additional bits of evidence have been discovered which have lent credence to the Indian story and have deepened the mystery and have fanned the treasure hunter's fever.

Lewis and Clark wrote of a light-skinned Indian with reddish hair and freckles that they met on the coast, indicating that the area may have had earlier visitors from Europe.

The Indians brought large quantities of beeswax to the early English and American trading posts. This was considered as evidence that there had been early shipwrecks in the Nehalem area where they said the beeswax came from.

In about 1890, a treasure hunter named Pat Smith found a marked rock, just as the Indians had said was used to mark the way to the treasure chest. Since then, hundreds of smaller marked rocks have been found in the vicinity. Many believe these rocks are clues giving directions to the treasure.

However, Dwayne Jensen, director of the Tillamook County Museum, who has made an intensive study of the the whole Neahkahnie mystery, along with Don Miles of Garibaldi, does not believe there is, or ever was, a Neahkahnie treasure chest of gold. Jensen and Miles have helped survey the mountain, and have kept track of hundreds of marked rocks (some of which are on display at the Tillamook Museum) and they have a different theory.

They say the markings on the rocks are survey marks, probably from a survey made by Sir Frances Drake in 1579. The marks and the distance between the mounds are measured in English yards, according to Jensen.

"The area bounded by the marked stones, which also indicate North and South, covers one square mile," Jensen reports. He adds that Drake was probably surveying to lay claim to the area for the British.

Jensen's research has led him to believe that the beeswax found in abundance near Nehalem was from a Spanish

Galleon wrecked there around 1595 or possibly from the ship of San Francisco Xavier, which disappeared in 1707.

There are other theories about the Neahkanie gold, too. One report says Astor's men from the Astoria post got it and packed it off.

Another bit of speculation indicates that William McKay, step-son of John McLoughlin, the Hudson Bay Factor, found the gold and kept it, distributing it freely to all in need in his later years.

One of the most persistent gold seekers over the years was a Pat Smith, who found the first marked rock. He was obsessed with searching for the treasure, even to marrying an old Clatsop Indian woman in hopes of getting more information from the tribe. Smith began to dig about 1870, and he was still at it in 1915.

Other gold seekers over the years included some Spaniards, who claimed to have special information about the treasure's whereabouts. They, too, gave up the search after a time and went home.

In 1931, two treasure seekers lost their lives on Neahkahnie Mountain when a deep hole they were digging caved in on them.

To add to the Neahkahnie mystery, two bronze handles that could have been from a treasure chest were found high and dry on the mountain when a tree stump was removed. The handles and a piece of wax were imbedded deeply under the roots. Did this mean that someone had found the gold years earlier and discarded the handles under the tree? And how did the wax get in such a place?

The Nehalem sandpit and Neahkahnie Mountain have kept their secret well. The land has passed through different hands since the white men took possession, and most of the owners have permitted digging for the treasure to continue. So many holes have been dug that Neahkahnie Mountain is sometimes called "The Mountain of a Thousand Holes." Now the land is partly in private ownership and partly owned by the State Parks System.

Sacajawea

Princes Angelina

Narcissa Whitman

Bethenia Owens-Adair

DID WOMEN WIN NORTHWEST?

Women Get Credits

Take the women out of Northwest history and you raise some big questions about how things would have turned out for Oregon, Washington and Idaho.

Contemplate the possible consequences—the Lewis and Clark Expedition might have failed without Sacajawea's help. The Hudson Bay Company men, the first white residents in the Northwest, would very likely have all been scalped if it hadn't been for their Indian wives.

Oregon, Washington and Idaho with the British Hudson Bay Company firmly entrenched, probably would have gone to Britain and be part of Canada today, if all those American women hadn't risked their lives coming West in covered wagons to start homes here and establish the United States' right to the country.

Even though most historians concede that women did play an important role in the Northwest, women got little credit earlier and did not even get to vote here for more than 50 years after they arrived in goodly numbers. For the most part, early Northwest women remain unsung heroines.

Sacajawea came along with the Lewis and Clark Expedition to the mouth of the Columbia River in 1805 mostly by accident. However, it was a fortunate accident for the expedition. She was a Shoshone Indian who had been taken captive as a child by another tribe and had either been bought as a slave or won in a gambling game by Toussaint Charbonneau, a guide. Charbonneau decided when he was hired by Lewis and Clark to make the trip west that he would bring Sacajawea along instead of his other wife because she had a new baby that she could carry. The other wife's child was older and couldn't be easily toted.

A chance meeting with Sacajawea's brother, a Shoshone chief, while en route through the Rockies, gave the pathfinders friendly passage through hostile country. Many times during the long trek Sacajawea proved invaluable to the expedition. Once, when a canoe overturned in a swift stream, she was credited with saving not only herself and her baby, but also valuable supplies. Lewis said that the expedition could not have proceeded without these things.

Jane Barnes, a British barmaid, reputed to be the first white woman to set foot in the Northwest, arrived by ship in 1813 with Donald McTavish, who was to be governor at the fur trading post of Astoria. Jane, who had bought a fine wardrobe for the journey, paraded on the beaches in her finery and impressed the Indians.

When McTavish drowned a month after their arrival, the son of Clatsop Chief Concomly offered her his hand and lodge which she promptly refused. She departed soon afterwards for London by way of China.

The first two white women to come to the Northwest by the overland route and cross the Rockies were cut of different cloth. They were Eliza Spaulding and Narcissa Whitman.

Narcissa had strong religious convictions and wanted more than anything to be a missionary to Western American Indians. When told that a single woman could not be assigned to this task, she promptly married Rev. Marcus Whitman, and in 1836 the Whitmans and the Spauldings set out from St. Louis for the Oregon Country.

The trip was a rough one because there was no wagon route to follow, and Mrs. Spaulding was sickly, but Narcissa was enthusiastic and optimistic. Settling at Waiilatpu, the Whitmans served as mission leaders until massacred in 1847 by the Indians they had come to help.

History sometimes remembers Marcus Whitman as a controversial figure, but praises Narcissa for her sunny disposition, her hard work and her boundless enthusiasm. Besides that, she was quite pretty and well educated.

Perhaps the greatest unsung heroines in the story of

Northwest settlement are the thousands of women who left their homes and traveled the wagon train route to the Pacific Coast. The trip frequently involved hardships hard to imagine. It took about six months or more, and many women died en route to be buried in shallow graves. In the summer it was hot and dusty; Indian attacks were frequent; in the winter it was unbearably cold and wet in the flimsy wagons. Some starved; some died of cholera. Some women had babies en route; some lost their husbands and found themselves alone in a strange land with hungry children to support.

Those who made it didn't have any picnic after they arrived. When they reached The Dalles, overland immigrants had to place their wagons on rafts to proceed down the Columbia by water. Here a bottleneck developed as hundreds of wagons sought transportation. Food was short and in desperation, many started out on makeshift rafts for a trip down the river that turned into a nightmare. One woman wrote that the icy water was knee-deep over their raft, as they were buffeted along with sleet and snow beating down on them and everything in the wagons soaking wet.

One of the women who made the overland trip to Oregon in the Applegate wagon train in 1843 was Bethenia Owens, who was a small child at the time. Determined to get an education, she worked hard for funds for schooling— picking berries, washing and ironing and finally opening a millinery establishment in Roseburg.

When she was 30-years-old, she finally managed to get to medical school, and she returned to Roseburg as the first woman graduate physician on the Pacific Coast.

Not accepted by her fellow physicians and anxious to prove her skills equal to theirs, she had to leave town after her male counterparts taunted her into performing an autopsy on a male cadaver. This shocked the community so badly that she moved to Portland, where she became a successful physician. She also practiced in Yakima. Later, she toured Europe and studied in hospitals in Scotland,

London, Paris and Berlin.

Always out-spoken, Bethenia returned to the Northwest to again shock by advocating the sterilization of habitual criminals and feeble-minded. In 1905 such a law was enacted, but defeated later by court action.

As the Pacific Northwest's first woman physician, Bethenia Owens-Adair paved the way for women professionals and proved equal to professional survival in the face of great opposition.

During the Indian Wars of 1855-58, a number of Indian women distinguished themselves by acts of bravery which resulted in the saving of lives, often with the risk of their own lives.

Princess Angelina, daughter of Seattle Chief Sealth, helped carry messages that may have saved the settlement of Seattle from disaster when it was attacked by an overwhelming number of Indians.

Winema, a Modoc Indian Princess, daughter of Chief Se-cut, proved to be as fearless as her name implied (Wi-ne-ma interpreted as "brave heart"). She played a notable part in the Modoc rebellion, acting as messenger and interpreter and saving the life of Col. A. B. Meacham at the risk of her own, and afterwards nursing him to health.

The Indian wife of James Birnie, who was the Hudson Bay manager at Fort George (Astoria), deserves special mention in any list of important Northwest women because she ushered in a kind of women's liberation for Indian wives of white men. While most of the Hudson Bay men married to Indians kept their wives in the background, and made them eat at the second table or in the kitchen, Mrs. Birnie, a daughter of Chief Concomly, would have none of such treatment. She presided at her husband's table as hostess in high style and took an active part in business affairs.

However, once a year she reverted to being an Indian and in her grand canoe with a cadre of oarsmen, whe swept down the river and spent a month camping on Willapa Bay where she directed the gathering and drying of berries, fish, oysters and other provisions.

Mary Got the Cash

Mary Montgomery, mother of three, an early Northwest resident with a forceful personality, made a wild, rush trip to Portland in 1873 to talk a banker out of $60,000 in cash to save a railroad.

The railroad was the Northwest Pacific which was trying to complete a portion of its line from Kalama to Puget Sound before its charter ran out on December 19.

Mary's husband, James Montgomery from Pennsylvania, was a 38-year-old journalist who had abandoned his pen in favor of contracting and high finance. He had won the railroad construction contract and Mary came west with him and she brought some style to the backwoods country and what is now the Chehalis Prairie.

Mary didn't live in a log cabin like most pioneer housewives, but had her household in two large tents and a shake wanigan. One tent housed the children and their nurse, another was Mary's domain and the wanigan served as kitchen and shelter for her Chinese cook.

When there was a construction crisis to meet the December deadline and payroll money failed to arrive from the east because the railroad, like everything else, was hard hit by the growing recession of 1873, Montgomery told his wife there would be trouble with the workers if he could not get $60,000 in cash to pay the crews by Sunday. They were getting restive and threatening to quit.

It was agreed that Mary was the logical person and the only one that could be trusted to make the speedy trip to Portland, explain the problem to the bank and return with the cash.

Mary left on horseback on Friday morning, riding her horse 10 miles to the railroad. From there the construction train gave her a ride in the cab alongside the engineer to the Toutle River where she caught the passenger train to Kalama.

At Kalama she had to transfer to a steamer enroute from Astoria to Portland. She arrived in Portland that night after the banks were closed, so she went directly to the home of the bank president, who finally agreed to meet her the next morning at the dock with the money sacks.

He was late and the only steamer for Astoria had cast off before Mary could get aboard, but the captain shouted at her to board the boat to The Dalles and said she could transfer to his ship at the mouth of the Willamette River.

When the steamers were brought alongside, a gangplank was laid between them and Mary had to walk it to reach the deck of the steamer to Astoria.

Disembarking at Kalama, she climbed back on her horse and leading another loaded with the money, she reached camp after dark Saturday night. The Sunday payroll was met.

1910 Palimony Suit

The Northwest's first "palimony suit" didn't take place last year in Baker, as reported in current newspaper headlines. It was filed in Portland in 1910.

That was the year that Ora Bramhill, who had lived with Arelas I. Agnew of Columbia Optical Company for 12 years, filed suit in Circuit Court for $1,800 against the estate of Agnew.

Agnew had died, leaving no provision for Ms. Bramhall in his will, but the woman said she was entitled to the $1,800 because that was the balance owed her under a contract that she and Agnew had drawn prior to his death.

The duly signed contract, presented in court, was labeled by the *Oregonian* reporting the case, as "a strange contract." It said:

Ora Bramhall and Arelas I. Agnew had lived together for 12 years and that each held the highest esteem for the other.

In all the years of their relationship, it added, there never had been any mutual agreement of promises of marriage between them.

Both parties to the agreement said if they were to separate at some future date, "neither would molest, or interfere, or intrude, or annoy the other in any way, shape or form, providing the provision for the payments herein mentioned are made as agreed."

Then the contract got specific and said, "I, Arelas I. Agnew, in consideration of the good and friendly services of Ora Bramhall, who has cared for me, cooked and nursed me in sickness, and in consideration of her love and affection, I agree to pay $6,000, with $1,000 paid upon signing of the contract and $100 a month to be paid until payment in full is made."

The contract added that Agnew and his heirs were bound by the contract, and that if Ora Bramhall should die first Agnew would pay her funeral expenses. But Agnew died first and his heirs didn't want to pay.

No record can be found as to the outcome of this palimony case, but attorneys consulted by this reporter say the woman presenting the signed contract probably won her case and the $1,800, if the heirs didn't pay up in an out-of court settlement.

Nedless to say, the Bramhill-Agnew case made headline in the local papers and must have created quite a sensation in 1910!

Women Started Flax Industry

Two women are credited with introducing the flax industry in the Northwest, and for a time it looked as if flax would be a leading industry here.

In the early 1840's, a Mrs. Owens brought the first flax plants west of the Rockies when she planted some flax seeds at Clatsop. From the flax that she grew from those seeds, she made fiber and strong twine that she traded to the Indians for fish, game and protection for herself and her family.

A few years later, in 1844, another pioneer woman, Mrs. John Kirkwood, successfully sowed a field near Tualatin with fiber flax that she had brought across the plains. Her crop harvested, she proceeded to process the flax by hand and spun and wove it into clothing and household linens. However, it wasn't until 1876 that the fine quality of Oregon grown flax was recognized. That year, a Mr. Miller from Turner, Oregon, entered some flax he had grown in the Centennial Exposition at Philadelphia. The Oregon flax won a bronze medal and a certificate of excellence because of its superlative length, fine gloss and silky quality.

Impressed by the flax grown in the Northwest United States, an Irish Company decided to send representatives here to grow flax. They left two years later after their entire crop was destoyed by fire.

By 1888 one flax mill was established in Albany, Oregon that produced linen twines and thread. For the next 15 years, flax was mainly grown for seed, and the valuable flax straw was burned to get rid of it.

Then, the Oregon Women's Flax Association was formed at the insistence of the governor's wife, Mrs. W. P. Lord, to try to help advance the flax industry.

In 1915, the Oregon Legislature appropriated $50,000 for the establishment and maintenance of a flax plant at the state penitentiary to provide employment for inmates and a marketing facility for flax growers. Appropriations were required for a number of years to keep the mill in operation, but the mill eventually proved that properly processed flax could find a ready market. But it also proved that a worldwide market for Oregon could not be opened by means of convict labor.

About 1927, the state flax mill began operating at a profit and it was an excellent source of revenue for the state treasury for many years. However, legal problems developed in marketing flax processed by convicts and in 1935 Governor Martin appointed the Oregon Flax Committee to investigate the industry and make recommendations regarding its needs.

To solve the problems, three WPA financed flax plants were built in Lane, Marion and Clackamas Counties. And just in time, too. World War II, starting in 1941, greatly increased the demand for flax fibers far beyond the capacity of even the new plants. The interruption of production in other countries and the demand for flax fiber to fill military requirements sent the need for Northwest flax soaring. Ten more mills were constructed quickly with private and federal funds.

Within 5 years after the close of the war, 10 of the 14 processing flax plants had closed. Poor marketing practices, inadequate grading and sorting and the introduction of synthetic fibers spelled the doom of the Oregon flax industry.

Bloomer Lady Climbs Rock

A determined woman in "tennis shoes, short skirt and bloomers" was hailed as the first woman to scale the defiant cliffs and precipices of Castle Rock (Beacon Rock) on the Washington side of the Columbia River in 1901!

Mrs. Berta Smith of Portland, made the ascent of the 1146 foot high Beacon Rock, along with her husband and two other men in one hour and 17 minutes. It took her and the rest of the party 49 minutes to get back down.

The group left Portland on the OR&N Railroad armed with drills, hammers, long iron pipes and ropes on August 24, 1901. They stayed overnight at Columbia Beach and were discouraged because there was a heavy rain the next morning. Finally, when the rain slacked, a sailboat took them to the trail leading to the rock.

The ascent was even more difficult because the rocks were wet and slippery, according to reports. At one point near the top, a 30 foot vertical cliff had to be scaled hand-over-hand up a rope put in place by Smith, the climb leader. Ten feet from the summit, a narrow wedge-like ledge had to be walked for 30 feet to the base of the pinnacle that is the peak.

"A misstep would plunge the climber 1136 feet to the Columbia," a report of the climb stated.

Mrs. Smith, who followed her husband up the rock, required no assistance. She was the first one down the life rope when making the descent, the report concludes.

Madame Damnable Routs Army

"Madam Damnable," a stout Irishwoman with a strong rock throwing arm, a vile tongue and a bad temper got her name in Seattle in 1855 when she and her three vicious dogs kept a road-building crew in terror for a week.

Following the Indian attack on Seattle in October, 1855, when an estimated 2,000 Indians almost succeeded in wiping out the small settlement, it was decided that the clearing of land and building of roads was necessary if further defense of the city was to be accomplished.

In South Seattle, the road had to pass the boarding house kept by the hefty and volatile Irishwoman. For some reason, unknown to them, the madame hated the entire crew of the Decatur, the crew designated as the roadbuilders.

"Madame Damnable was a terrible woman and a terror to our people who found her tongue more to be dreaded than the entire Indian army recently encamped in our front," wrote an officer in charge of the roadwork.

Each crew working on that road carefully avoided that part that passed in front of the "female dragon's" house, until it was the only part of the project unfinished.

"Every imaginable device was adopted to complete this road, but the moment our men approached the scene, Madame Damnable with the three dogs at her heels would come tearing from her house, her apron filled with rocks. The way stones, rocks and curses flew was something fearful to contemplate. Charging like fury, the dogs were anxious to sink their teeth in the flesh of the detested invaders. Invariably, the division gave way before the storm, fleeing, officers and all, as if Old Satan himself were after them."

The first and second divisions failed in the attempt to build the road by the boarding house. When it became the third division's turn to try, no barrage greeted them at first and they were making good progress and congratulating themselves. Probably the "old dragon" was away, they decided.

"Then, suddenly, the door flew open and this demon in petticoats shot out upon us like a bolt from a catapult.

"Set upon with sticks, stones, curses and dogs, the division wavered, and then broke and fled in every direction," the officer said.

The captain of the ship decided the road had to be finished at any cost, but having felt the full weight of Madam Damnable's vituperative tongue, he did not wish another encounter and ordered his subordinates "to do their duty," without telling them "how to do it."

Finally, after various schemes failed, "two old salts" led a crew to the site. When Madam Damnable began her assault, these two stood their ground, and one of them tried to talk to her, to convince her of the importance of the protection to the town, and to the security of her property, and of their intent not to disturb or molest her.

His speech was interrupted and cut short by a piece of wood aimed at his head and by a torrent of abuse.

Then the other man, who had also held his ground, broke in.

"What do you mean, you darned old harridan, raising hell this way? I know you, you old curmudgeon. Many's the time I've seen you howling thunder at Fells Point, Baltimore. You're a damn pretty one, ain't you?"

The effect was magical. With a look of hatred, Madam Damnable turned and fled into her house with her dogs and was never seen again by the road builders, the officer said.

However, the road past her house, which should have taken two or three hours to complete, had consumed more than a week's time.   ❖

Grandma Brown

One of the best-hearted women who helped settle the West was a widow who had worked hard to support three children and who didn't start to the Northwest in a covered wagon until she was 66 years old.

Tabitha Moffat Brown, better known as "Grandma Brown" after she arived here, was born in Massachusetts in 1780. She became the widow of the Rev. Clark Brown, an Episcopal minister, in 1817. When she was 66 years old, in 1846, she crossed the plains to Oregon with a son and other members of her family. On the Scott-Applegate trail, the wagon train encountered much hardship and a brother-in-law died en route.

When Tabitha settled in West Tualatin, she found some 15 or 16 orphans of immigrants; these she gathered into a school, using a log church situated on what later became the west campus of Pacific University.

Today, Tabitha "Grandma" Brown is credited with the founding of Pacific University because her little school was the humble beginning of the University.

At first, Grandma Brown simply taught her orphans the three R's and how to cook, sew, and perform other useful tasks. In this work she was aided by The Rev. Harvey Clark and his wife.

In 1848, when Tualatin Academy was established, Grandma stayed on as school mother. A tiny lady, generous and self-sacrificing, she was much beloved by those whose lives she touched.

Courtesy Oregon Historical Society

Lady-Like Justice?

In the early days in the Northwest, the women, as well as the men, sometimes took justice into their own hands.

One such case occurred on the Oregon Coast when a Mrs. Radabaugh of Arago vigorously applied a horsewhip to a woman who had been preaching a new kind of religion in the Coquille Valley in 1908.

The incident was fully reported in the September 4 issue of the area paper, the Myrtle Point *Enterprise.*

It seems the female preacher had so influenced the 16-year-old Radabaugh daughter that the girl burned her best dresses and destroyed a watch that she had been given that she might sanctify herself according to the teachings of the new faith.

Mrs. Radabaugh was incensed and hunted up the woman preacher and demanded that she pay for the property destroyed, but the preacher made her way to the boat that carried passengers up and down the river and got away from the infuriated mother.

Not to be so easily defeated, Mrs. Radabaugh took a horse and buggy and followed the boat downstream to Coquille where she caught the preacher and again gave her a chance to pay for the destroyed property.

The woman would not pay and Mrs. Radabaugh proceeded to apply a horsewhip over her shoulders and body, finally knocking her down.

"The woman left by the first boat from the lower river point, probably thinking she was entitled to be classed with the prophets of old, who were beaten and tortured.

"But many others think she got what she deserved and hope that Mrs. Radabaugh's prompt action will make future visits of her ilk unpopular here," the *Enterprise* concluded.

MOTHER NATURE'S HAND

1880 Mini Hurricane

An estimated 325 fishermen drowned on the Oregon Coast off the Columbia River and Willapa Bay on May 4, 1880. And about 240 fishing boats were destroyed.

The morning of that May day seemed like a typical mild spring day. A gentle breeze was blowing, and conditions seemed ideal for commercial fishing. Almost every boat in the area went out trolling for salmon or dragging for bottom fish. They spread out over a 35-mile area around the mouth of the river.

There was no warning that a freak storm was about to hit. Without warning, a powerful wind of hurricane force suddenly came out of nowhere and pounded the calm ocean into massive waves. Winds of more than 100 miles an hour quickly capsized or swamped most of the 250 boats in the path of the storm.

Terrified fishermen were tossed into the towering swells. Death came quickly to most.

Although most coastal storms in the Northwest come from the southwest, this furious mini-hurricane came out of the Northwest. Few places on the shore were touched by the storm, which blasted the off-shore area for about 30 minutes. After half an hour of indescribable destruction and chaos, the storm ended almost as quickly as it had begun.

For days, the ocean beaches were covered with mute evidence of the destruction — dead bodies, splinters of wood, nets, and fishing gear. The 1880 tragedy was one of the worst ever recorded in the United States.

Meteor in Back Yard

A falling meteor dazzled the Northwest night sky on April 26, 1903, and frightened people from Seattle and Tacoma and as far south as Eugene.

In the Puget Sound area, it was reported to be so bright it illuminated the heavens like a full moon.

Moving from East to West, it was seen at an altitude of about 45 degrees and it seemed to explode and break into fiery pieces. An explosion was heard about three minutes later, which the weather bureau said indicated that the meteor exploded at 37 miles distance.

In Lake Oswego, Charles Weltner, a bartender at the Reception Salon, was home with his wife when he heard a hissing noise and then a terrific crack that sounded like the explosion of a cannon. The people in the neighborhood were so startled that they were afraid to leave their houses.

When they did get courage to go outside, they saw a red hot missile lying in the Weltner backyard. It was glowing red and lit up the whole backyard, the Weltners said.

Weltner brought a piece of the meteor to work with him the next day, and gave a piece to L. L. Hawkins for the City Museum. Other pieces were said to be found on the Eastside of Portland near 26th and Sandy.

Although several scientists questioned that the material found was really meteor, others believed them to be authentic and the Lake Oswego neighbors swore they were. The piece in the Weltner yard was completely oxidized carbon about 16 inches square, and weighed about 15 pounds.

Describing the event, the weather service report said, "A What-Was-It broke loose from its moorings among the planets eons ago and flew over the Northwest last night to end its long journey. It shook house and windows, and jammed telephone lines.

North Sister on left and Broken Top in distance may be rims of ancient Mt. Multnomah.

Pre-Historic Giant Mountain

The Three Sisters sit majestically in the Cascade Range, a landmark in the Northwest. The North Sister is very old, while the Middle and South Sister are very young peaks geologically.

No similar grouping of peaks is to be found anywhere else in the world, and the phenomena has been the subject of violent disagreement among scientists since the early 1900's.

Were the Three Sisters once part of a giant prehistoric mountain dubbed Mount Multnomah by scientists, which blew its top much like Mt. St. Helens did and left the remnant, North Sister? Then later, did the Middle and South Sister rear their heads in much the same volcanic fashion as dome building now going on at Mt. St. Helens?

This is the theory set forth in 1925 by Professor Edwin T. Hoage of the University of Oregon, who published a booklet entitled, *Mt. Multnomah, Ancient Ancestor of the Three Sisters.*

However, in 1944, another scientist, Howel Williams of the University of California published another brochure, entitled *Volcanoes of the Three Sisters Region, Oregon Cascades,* which called the Mt. Multnomah theory a myth. Williams said Mt. Multnomah never existed.

If Mt. Multnomah did exist, it was estimated to be at least 15,000 feet high, which would make it the tallest peak of the Cascades as we know them. The early Indians referred to the part of the Willamette River from the falls at Oregon City to the Columbia as "The Multnomah." These Indians were themselves known as Multnomas, which probably was a corruption of the word, "nemallomaq," meaning "downstream," according to early translations.

Geologists looking for a name for the prehistoric mountain decided Mt. Multnomah was appropriate.

Although these geologists say they can't be sure whether the top of the ancient mountain, if it did exist, was blown away or whether it subsided into the crater when upward pressure of gases and magma was reduced, the evidence is in favor of the theory that it disappeared in a volcanic explosion.

Today, there remains a portion of the great rim of the caldera that could have been left when the mountain blew away, the diameter of this caldera is about 8 miles, which makes it among the largest calderas in the world.

The peaks known as North Sister, Little Brother, the Sphinx and Broken Top are all older and are all parts of the ancient rim, according to the geologists who hold the Mt. Multnomah theory. They say that proof that the interior peaks within the caldera are all younger in age geologically substantiates their Mt. Multnomah theory.

Daring Sea Captain

An Oregon cave, said by some to be the world's largest sea cave of its type, was discovered by a retired sea captain, who risked his life in 1880 to explore it.

Captain William Cox discovered the opening to the cave, which is 10 miles south of Cape Perpetua, and laid daring plans to enter it by skiff, there being no known way to gain entrance from the land.

Perhaps he visioned that the cave held some ancient Spanish treasure loot from a captured galleon, or he might have thought a mermaid lived there. In any case, he decided to challenge the pulsating sea at the cave entrance in a small skiff.

With his heart in his mouth, he caught a large swell, and somehow managed to keep his craft from broaching and capsizing. The swell caught his boat and pushed it forward. Suddenly he found himself in almost total darkness. Lighting a kerosene lantern, he was amazed at the size and extent of the unusual cavern where he had landed.

Cox was excited. He knew he was the first white man to enter this strange, hidden domain. Probably no coastel Indian ever entered it either, because they believed such places to be filled with evil spirits.

Exploring the two acres of floor and the vaulted ceilings, which rose 125 feet high, Cox failed to notice the mounting surf foaming and curling at the entrance. A few sea lions barked at him; he went on exploring.

When he finally decided to leave, his passageway out was blocked. He was trapped. The ocean was mounting with the fury of an approaching storm.

The adventurer had no alternative but to settle down with

his sea lion companions. Soon he was cold and damp and hungry, but there was no way out. Several days later the seas calmed, and the desperate Captain Cox made a daring exit through the surf.

As a reward for his derring-do, it would have seemed appropriate that the cave be named in honor of Cox, but it was not. Today it is known as Sea Lion Cave. The only thing named for Cox is a prominent seamount, a conical hunk of basalt about a mile and a half south of Heceta Head. ❖

Impressive Volcanic History

With Mt. St. Helens erupting and continuing its quaking, shaking and volcanic jiggle dance, most Northwest residents are finally convinced — we do live on the Pacific rim of fire!

Before St. Helens started acting up, most citizens of Washington and Oregon thought of volcanic activity as something that had happened in pre-historic times. However, a look at Northwest history tells us differently.

Old records, diaries, and newspaper articles tell the story of a number of eruptions of the mountains in the Northwest's Cascade Range during the past 150 years. Although most of the eruptions evidently were minor, they still make an impressive list.

Here are the best documented reports:

Mt. Rainier — Nov. 13, 1843; Oct. 19, 1873 for 7 days; May, 1880; 1884, steam for 2 hours; 1894, columns of black smoke and jets of steam.

Mt. Baker — Jan. 1853; summer 1854; Dec. 1880, 1842 and continuing on and off from 1846 to 1860. The earliest climbers reported finding a blast area with trees flattened much like the devastation found on Mt. St. Helens. The date of such a blast is not known, but it is presumed to have been in the early 1800's.

Mt. St. Helens — 1831; 1842; 1843, an eruption lasting 85 days; 1854, 70 days. Also in 1841, 1846, 1852 and 1970s 1980s.

Mt. Jefferson — blew smoke and steam in 1894.

Mt. Hood — 1846; 1854; 1859, 2 days; 1865, 15 days; 1869, a 3-hour eruption; and in Sept. 1859, two men bringing cattle across the Cascades reported a column of fire from the mountain which continued for two hours during the night. At daylight, the snowfields on the mountain were black.

Chief Joseph

INDIANS WERE FIRST

Northwest Pocahontas

The Northwest has its own "Pocahontas" story, although it is not as well known as the Eastern Seaboard version.

There has been much speculation about how the Coquille Indians who lived in what is now Coos County on the Oregon Coast got their name.

The most logical explanation seems to be that a French sea captain, who was the first white navigator to enter the waters of the Coquille River, bestowed it upon them.

He observed about 500 Indians in this tribe. They seemed to live mostly on great amounts of shellfish and mussels which they gathered in abundance.

The French word for mussells is Coquille, so he named both the river and the tribe, "Coquille."

The last chief of all the tribes in the area was Chief Washington, who lived at the foot of Sugar Loaf Mountain. Before the white men settled the coast, these tribes lived in an Indian paradise. Game of all kinds was plentiful. There were lots of fish and berries, and the climate was mild.

Every year the Selawaw people from what is now Multnomah County would come to hunt with the Coquilles. The big hunts were for elk, and the Indians would dig holes 5 or 6 feet deep and plant sharpened sticks in the center. Then they would cover the holes with boughs, surround the herds of elk and start driving them toward the pits.

The best of the buck elks would be in the lead and would break through into the pits, spear themselves and become easy prey to the hunters.

An Indian chief's daughter, who was willing to risk her life for the white man she loved, saved a number of white settlers from an untimely death and she won the man she loved.

When Ephriam Catchin moved to the Coquille River Valley on the Oregon Coast in the early 1800's, he gained the reputation of being a peaceful paleface. The Indians were not averse to being friendly to such men, and Ephraim had good qualities and was tall, athletic and handsome.

Catchin was trapping near the Indians and soon began trying to teach them the language of King George men (as the white men were called). To his best Indian scholars, Ephriam added writing and reading. His best pupil was the daughter of the chief, who soon learned to speak, read and write English.

Gradually, more white men came to the valley, built houses and squatted. Relations between the white men and the Indians became uneasy, as the Indians saw their lands being taken over.

Then a white man's body was found in a slough (afterwards known as Dead Man's Slough). Shortly afterwards, it was reported that blankets were seen at an Indian camp that formerly had been carried by the unknown dead man.

Tim Terman, being the only duly elected official in the area, decided to act as sheriff and raised a well-armed posse that was still better supplied with fire water, according to a report in the *Myrtle Point Enterprise,* which wrote of the incident many years later.

Arriving at the Indian camp, the posse found only two old men and a 12-year-old boy present. The old men escaped, but the boy, not fearing whites, remained. In a wild shooting skirmish that ensued as the two old men made their escape, the boy was hit in the hip by a reckless shot. He fell begging for his life, but every man of the posse emptied his rifle and killed the boy as revenge.

Following this incident, the Coquille Indians rose against the whites and made a plot with the Rogue Indians who were already on the warpath. They swore the extermination of all the white men in the area.

The chief's daughter, who had earlier been taught to

speak and write English by Catchin, had fallen in love with her teacher and she was able to warn him of the plot through a letter that she managed to get to him.

Heeding the warning, Catchin and his neighbors hastily built a log house, surrounded by barricades. It was located on a hill and was well stocked with provisions to withstand a siege.

Again, the Indian girl, now suspected of treachery by the tribe, slipped away to inform Catchin that attack was imminent. He notified all the settlers to come to the fort so they could safely fight together.

The next morning, the fort was attacked and the Indians repulsed with the loss of several men.

After the attacking Indians had left, the girl appeared outside the fort and claimed protection from Catchin, saying the Indians would kill her. Catchin was averse to having her at the fort, and told her that taking her in was not possible.

Grief-stricken and panic-stricken, the girl left the fort and tried to kill herself by hanging from a tree. Catchin, hearing the commotion, ran out and cut her down, exclaiming that a girl trying to give her life for his sake was good enough to become his wife.

When the siege was over, Catchin took his bride-to-be to meet his mother who lived in the Willamette Valley. The mother was surprised and shocked when her son turned up with the Princess, but after hearing the story, she agreed to the marriage and the ceremony was performed in her home.

Frances Catchin, the Indian girl who now had two new names, was well liked by the settlers and was gladly accepted by their wives. She was always modest, neat, clean and hospitable and she and Catchin had four children. About 10 years after her marriage, she contracted "consumption" and died. �֎

Capture Leads to Romance

In 1854, three young German youths disembarked when the steamer on which they were traveling to the Northwest stopped at the mouth of the Chetco River in Oregon to take on fresh water.

The youths were curious about the country and decided to have a look around. Neither they nor the captain of the ship knew that the Southern Oregon Indians were on the warpath and in an ugly mood.

The three had hardly landed when they were captured by the Chetco Indians, who planned to kill the three whites.

The young Germans thought for sure they were doomed, but that night a 12-year-old Indian girl and her 13-year-old brother crept up and managed to release the three. They hid the frightened youths near the shore.

Realizing that his three passengers had been captured by the Indians, the captain of the ship did not know what to do. He knew he could not risk the danger of sending a rescue party to search for them because they would be far outnumbered by the Indians.

For several days, the Germans stayed in hiding along the shore. The two Indian youngsters were able to smuggle food to their white friends, but the three could not figure out how to get to the ship so they could be rescued.

Finally, the Indian boy was able to take his canoe out to the ship, and carry a message to the captain. A boat was then sent to shore that night to pick up the three.

The ship then continued on to Port Orford where the three Germans lived for awhile. Finally, they decided to return to Germany. By this time, the Indian wars were over and the Indians were friendly, so the three prevailed upon the ship's captain to stop at the Chetco river, so they could again disembark and look around at the place where they had spent an anxious time.

The same Indians were still living at the river mouth, and one of the Germans, Schmidt, sought out Skamamaktra, the little Indian girl who had saved his life. She had grown into a beautiful young lady and he fell in love with her and decided to stay in Oregon after she told him that she knew he would come back for her.

The other two Germans, Koch and Ringe, said they would stay, too. So the three told the captain of the ship farewell.

Schmidt and Skamamaktra were married by Indian rites, and after a few months they hiked to Crescent City, the closest place to obtain a marriage license, and were legally married there.

Returning to Gold Beach, the couple made their home for many years at Hunters Creek. ✢

First White Casualty

The first United States citizen north of the Columbia River to be killed by Indians was a visitor to the Hudson Bay Company post at Ft. Nisqually in 1846.

A party of Snoqualmie Indians made an attack on the fort that spring, and Leander Wallace accidently became the victim.

About 150 Indians under Patkanim came in force to the fort one day, ostensibly to settle a dispute with the Nisqually tribe. The chief was let within the fort to confer with Dr. Tolmie, the Hudson Bay agent, and the gates were closed to keep the rest of the Indians outside.

Three white men, who were visitors at the fort at the time, were outside the gates when they noticed that the Indians were making some hostile demonstrations. They became alarmed and sensing danger, made a run for the gates.

Unfortunately, when they reached the gates they were not opened by the guard on the inside. Instead, the guard fired a volley of shots into the air to try to scare off the Indians. Instead, the Indians took the shots to mean that the hostilities had begun and they fired upon Leander Wallace and the two other white men still outside the gates. Wallace was killed, and the other two were injured.

The Hudson Bay Company persuaded the Indians, several days later, to give up for trial the murderers who had fired the shots, in exchange for 8 blankets.

When the new governor of the territory, Lane, heard about the deal, he was incensed, but before he could intervene, the deal was consummated and 6 Snoqualmie Indians were turned in by the crafty Patkanim.

At a special court, hastily convened at Ft. Steilacoom, the

6 were indicted and two were convicted. The other four were acquitted. The trial lasted two days, and was attended by a large number of Indians, as was the execution of the two a couple of days later.

This was the first U.S. Court held north of the Columbia River. Some of the jurors rode over 200 miles to reach the court. It was presided over by Chief Justice Bryant. ❖

Jackson Sundown

Boy Buried Alive

Taking slaves captured from other tribes was a common practice among many of the Northwest Indians. A young boy, captured from the Klamath tribe, was made a slave and taken as a companion to the son of a Wasco chief.

The two little boys were good friends and the slave boy received the same treatment as the son of the chief. Then the chief's family became ill and all died except his small son, the slave boy's companion. Then the son died.

The chief sat in silence for 4 days by his son's bedside, not speaking. At last he gave the command that his son was to be prepared for burial and that the slave boy was to be buried alive with him.

The chief's son and the rest of the family were carried to the death house of the family on Memeloose, the burial island in the Columbia River. The vault was made of heavy planks, sodded up except for a small, low door.

The dead were piled in, and the slave boy who had been the son's constant companion and playmate, with the same privileges, was bound to the dead son with strong grass ropes. The vault was closed and sealed with rocks and dirt.

Indian Johnny, who was friendly with some nearby missionaries, heard about the burial of the live boy and he hurried to tell the missionaries. They were at the death house by dawn. They opened the door, removing the rocks and dirt that sealed the entrance and found the little slave boy, unconscious and in a pool of blood from struggling to free himself on the ropes, but he was alive. He had torn loose from his master, but the thongs had cut deeply into his skin.

Out in the fresh air, he regained consciousness and was carried to the mission house where his wounds gradually healed. The missionary, a Mrs. Perkins, adopted him and named him Georgie Waters. He eventually went to Jason Lee's missionary school near Salem in the Willamette Valley and then was sent east with Capt. John Fremont where he was educated at Columbia College in New York.

Georgie Waters returned to the Oregon Country was an evangilist and teacher and was ordained a Methodist missionary in Portland in 1871. He later moved to the Yakima area and was elected head chief of the Yakima Confederation on March 22, 1910. He died there.

Chief of Walla Wallas

Indian Ghosts

The Indians of the Northwest believed in ghosts. When the white men first arrived, they were surprised to find that ghosts played important roles in Indian lore. Not that these earlier white arrivals didn't have ghosts of their own to believe in, but the Indian ghosts were different.

Ghosts led interesting lives in Northwest Indian lore. Puget Sound Indians believed that a person's soul went with them to the land of the ghosts and their reputations followed.

When someone died the survivors collected all of the belongings of the deceased and placed them into the canoe with the body. If the survivors inadvertently kept any belongings of the dead person, the ghost would return and try to reclaim his possessions.

Indian ghosts could hunt, fish, travel and play. They lived in the West, and always across a river.

After death, the Indians thought the soul had a long road to travel if it was an extended illness. The road was short for an unexpected death. The soul always came to two rivers — one having a log bridge, the other dependent on catching the attention of another ghost to bring a canoe to pick them up.

Occasionally, someone who didn't like being a ghost would come back to continue their life or come back as a new baby.

Other tribes believed that a ghost always came back to sing to the house he had lived in. Some tribes were sure their tribe would all be in a special area of ghostdom.

Deceased ancestors were not worshipped, as they are in some countries, but were respected and survivors felt the dead were dependent on them. The Tlingit burned their dead so they couldn't be cold and sang to them, so they wouldn't be lonely.

Tlingit legend says if the deceased led a quiet, uneventful life and died a natural death, the afterlife would be the same. If the deceased was a warrior or a brave and died violently, he would go the sky and have much happiness. Bad Indians, they said, went down into the earth to darkness. ❖

Smelt Routs Tribe

In 1890, Indian smelt fishing impressed the early home-steaders. They were particularly impressed if during the runs they visited an Indian encampment and saw the thousands of fish painstakingly laid with heads landward to dry in the sun.

The Indians had a superstition that the fish must all be laid this way, with their heads pointing upstream or their spirits would return to the sea.

One night two teenage boys, sons of homesteaders, who had watched the Indians at the Alsea smelt-fishing grounds carefully place their catch as prescribed, decided to have some fun.

Under cover of night and the barking of the Indian dogs they crept into the Indian camp and changed all of the smelt to face seaward.

No one but the boys knew why the Indians all disappeared the next day, leaving their fish behind. Recalling the incident later, one of the youths said, "If the Indians had caught us, we'd have been scalped, and if my dad learned of it, we'd have been strapped on the rear."   ❖

Poem of Understanding

Ambitious early Northwest pioneers had trouble under-
standing relaxed ways of native Indians. A Seattle poet tried
to explain cultural differences and backgrounds.

The Siwash—From Seattle Sunday Times, 1906.

> Stolid he sits, the Siwash of the Sound
> Hard by the corner of the city street
> And heeds not any halt of hurrying feet
> Before his outspread mats and baskets browned
> And crude (yet curious patterned weaves abound)
> That make his tribal art unique, complete
> And if you turn to go, no tones entreat
> And if you buy, he sells in calm profound.
>
> The hustling white men look with fullest scorn
> Upon the unkept wanderers, silent grave;
> And few there are who pause to meditate
> Or pity give the Indians who are born
> To learn their day is past.
> Why speak?
> Why slave?
> The Siwash struggles not against his fate!
> *Alice Harriman*

Whale of a Tale

The Tillamook Indians had a strange way of fishing for whale in the early days, but a pioneer writing for the South Coos County American paper in 1925 recalls at least one time in 1863 when it worked.

Chief Sampson was head of the Tillamook Tribe of Indians at that time, and the tribe had grown tired of living on potatoes and salmon, two of their staple items of food. They wanted whale meat and oil, so the chief took the usual way of fishing for whale — a 10 day fast.

This fast was the chief's job, according to L. Strong, who was a friend of the tribe. The other Indians danced.

At last the chief had to lie down on a blanket, he was too weak from want of food to get up. Then on the next day, the 11th day, word came up from the mouth of the bay 15 miles away that a whale was stranded on the South Spit!

The Indians busily began transporting Mr. Whale to their store houses. Each squaw carried an 18-inch square of whale about a foot long and a foot or two thick. A pony could carry two such pieces.

When all the meat was stored in the shacks, the Indians used the large intestine for a container by tying the ends to a post and filling it with oil.

"Then they proceeded to drink the oil like tea or coffee, using large clam shells for cups," Strong recalls.

The whale fishing had been a great success and the chief ended his fast with a whale feast!

Coming of the Gypsy

No one is sure how or when the Rom, or gypsies, came to the Northwest, but old records tell about, and old-time residents remember, when caravans of gypsies traveled around the countryside. Gypsies also were remembered as always being part of the scene at carnivals, mining camps and in small towns.

Many stories and supersitions, probably brought here from Europe, surrounded the gypsies.

"They'll steal you blind," or, "They steal blond children," or, "Gypsies always steal chickens."

In many early day Northwest towns, the gypsies were run out at sunset. Then their campfires could be seen burning brightly at their camps just outside town.

The caravans of gypsies of later years, after they abandoned their horse-drawn wagons in favor of swifter transportation, usually consisted of eight to ten old-time touring cars loaded with an assortment of women in colorful and multiple skirts, revealing blouses and scarves, lots of half-naked children, and dark, thin men in rather ordinary dress.

When this entourage descended on a small country store, the storekeeper rushed to lock the door before they entered if he saw them coming. Although they always seemed to have money to spend, the gypsy women also were adept at concealing large amounts of merchandise in their voluminous skirts and it would have taken an army of clerks to watch each one as they swarmed over the place.

Today, gypsies in the Northwest have abandoned their nomadic way of life, and mostly live in old storefronts or vacant buildings in the downtown areas of the larger cities. A recent survey by a Gypsy leader indicates that there are still about 1,000 gypsies in Washington, and probably and equal number, or more, in Oregon. Today's gypsies are mostly invisible, except for the few who are fortune tellers and dress for the part.

Most of the gypsy men today are involved in the used car business. Many families are on welfare, but new gypsy leaders are coming forth and there is an attempt underway to push for more education for gypsies.

Many historians believe that the Rom came to the Northwest by wagon about the same time that pioneers and gold-seekers were making their way across the plains and over the mountain ranges. However, there are no records to substantiate this. ❖

N. W. Racism

In 1864, the Oregon Legislative Committee passed a law that slavery should not exist in Oregon. The committee which acted with full authority at that time for the Oregon territory also said any Negro slave brought to Oregon should become free within three years.

At the same time, the committee said any Negro or mulatto coming into the country should leave within two years. If he, or she, failed to do so, a whipping on the bare back with 30 lashes should be given every six months.

The following session, this law was repealed and the question of slavery was a controversial one for many years. In the meantime, a number of Oregon people held slaves.

When the Constitutional Convention met in Salem in 1857 to adopt the proposed constitution for the new State of Oregon, it was decided to include two issues for the people to decide at an election the next November. When the election was held, the voters voted 7,727 to 2,645 against slavery. The vote against free Negro residents was 8,640 to 1,081. This meant that Negroes would not be allowed to live in Oregon, but this provision was never enforced.

Much bitterness surrounded the ratification of the 14th Amendment of the federal Constitution, which conferred the privileges of citizenship on the recently freed Negroes following the Civil War. The Oregon Legislature did ratify the amendment, however, on September 12, 1866.

PLACES & HAPPENINGS

Seattle Burns

The greatest conflagration on the Pacific Coast was started in a Seattle cabinet-maker's shop when a can of spilled paint was ignited by a lantern.

It was between 2 and 3 p.m. in the afternoon of June 6, 1889, when the blaze began. By 5:30 p.m., twelve blocks of downtown Seattle and six wharves were already in ashes, and a few hours later, 40 city clocks and about half of the waterfront wharves were totally destroyed.

So hot was the blaze that not a single building inside the perimeter of the fire was saved.

The fire department was summoned when the blaze began and they arrived just as the fire was spreading into the wholesale liquor dealers upstairs above the cabinet shop. (The new Federal Building stands on this spot today.)

The firemen almost had the blaze extinguished when the water pressure in their hoses dropped and then quit altogether.

Almost immediately, the fire gained momentum and in minutes it burst out of the north end of the block.

Panic spread almost as fast as the fire. Telegrams were hastily sent to Tacoma, Portland, Port Townsend and Victoria requesting help. Frantic merchants grabbed what they could and ran to safety.

Wooden planks which were the city sidewalks and streets at the time aided the spread of the fire from block to block. Firemen, merchants and passersby frantically began tearing up planking.

Whole blocks were dynamited to try and stop the spreading blaze. Bucket brigades of 200 men extended from the salt water up the Seattle hills as far as Third Avenue.

Mostly their efforts were in vain. The surrounding cities responded to the calls of help, but most arrived too late. Seattle was burning and the wooden buildings and the wooden streets, along with the lack of water pressure to combat the blaze, turned the whole town into a raging inferno.

When the fire was finally stopped, everything from University Street on the north to Charles Street on the tideflats on the south and from the waterfront on the west to Third Avenue on the east was gone.

All the major shipping wharves, the newspaper, the opera house, lumber mills, and small businesses were out of business or they were without a building.

But Seattle was undaunted. Before the ashes were cold, most of the townspeople had gathered at the Armory, which was left standing, to plan the rehabilitation of their city.

One thing they all agreed on...no more wooden buildings. They resolved to set up codes to prohibit wooden structures in the core area of the city. They planned for a fireboat. They redesigned the sewer, water and street systems to cope with a much larger and more efficient city.

Some say the Seattle fire was the best thing that ever happened to Seattle. It not only united the different factions in a spirit of rebuilding, but it resulted in a good basic foundation for a new and better city. Gone were the ramshackle old buildings, the shacks, and much of the squalor that had previously predominated the town.

Taking spirit, most of the merchants resumed "business as usual" in makeshift locations while the rebuilding was underway. Tents sprang up in the ashes and many merchants reopened businesses immediately.

Within 30 days after the fire, 88 brick buildings were under construction. The pioneer spirit was alive and well and Seattle was off to a new start. ✜

Three-Level City

Oregon City, one of the earliest settlements on the Willamette River, is a three-decker town, and one of the few cities of the Northwest that boasts a public elevator to get residents from one level of town to another.

But when the controversial water-powered Oregon City elevator was finally put into operation in 1915, householders found their water faucets had gone dry. And the public drinking fountain across from the Everhart store in Elyville would not function when the elevator cage was on its way up the bluff.

The city Water Board that had fought the construction of the elevator was right! Oregon City did not have a good enough water supply to adequately supply the households and the elevator at the same time.

However, in spite of this handicap, it was reported that 3,869 persons rode the lift in one day, and the townspeople contended with the difficulty until 1924 when the elevator was finally converted to electricity.

Agitation for a public elevator in Oregon City had started as early as 1899. In 1874, the first steps were built up the bluff. These were hailed as an improvement over the slippery trails. The steps were better as a way to church than the "Baptist slide," one resident remarked. But the busy townspeople only talked about a lift for many years.

The first action for an elevator was taken by the City Council in 1912. An act was submitted to the voters of Oregon City for their approval of an elevator. It passed 687 to 433.

A committee called the "Livewires" was formed to work out the details and in 1913, an engineer was hired. However, bluff property owners were not enchanted with the idea of having an elevator anchored in their view property. The matter was finally taken to the Supreme Court and it was ruled that the city had the right to take a section of property for public use. The owner of the piece selected, a Mrs. Charles, received $1,651.20 for the site appropriated.

Later, in 1913, another bitter quarrel came into the open over the construction of the elevator. The elevator was designed to use water for power. The Board of Water Commissioners didn't think the town had an adequate water system to operate the elevator. The Council disagreed and tried to dissolve the Water Board. The Water Board would not be kicked out of office and again the issue went to court. This time the Circuit Court ruled that the council could appoint the board, but couldn't remove members from office.

In December, 1931, the elevator shaft was finished, but it remained a silent sentinel for two years. The Water Board and the Council were stalemated.

By July, 1915, the Council and the Water Board had a reconciliation, probably because of changed personnel. When the water-powered elevator was finished, it turned out the original Water Board was right, but the city had a water-powered elevator and it was used anyway.

For 41 years, the original elevator remained in service, until it was finally replaced by the present white column.

One of the most remarkable facts about the old elevator is that there was never an accident to either passenger or operators, say Oregon City records. ❖

Oysterville Preacher Tough

Oysterville, one of the first towns on the Washington Long Beach Peninsula, is a sleepy little settlement today, with a number of interesting historic houses built in the 1850-70's. But things were not always so quiet in Oysterville. For 32 years, Oysterville was the county seat; it had 2 hotels, 5 saloons, a weekly newspaper and even a college.

Before the white settlers came, the Indians gathered at Oysterville, harvested and dried Willapa Bay oysters. Then, in 1854, two men, a logger and a former New York tailor, discovered the oyster beds. They platted a town at the site and began packing oysters to ship to San Francisco.

Not long after the town was founded, the Indian War of 1855-56 broke out. The settlers at Oysterville started to build a log fort, which the friendly Chinook Indians regarded as a joke. The pioneers also decided it was a pretty silly thing to do, and they never finished it.

County government was sketchy, and there wasn't really any until 1869 when a tin box was purchased for $3 to store the assessor's records and a safe and a lot for a future courthouse was purchased. It was 1878 before a chair and a water pitcher was provided for the county judge. Expense accounts also include $15 for services of a crier for the court that had 3 trials on the docket that year. In addition, sawdust was purchased for the courtroom floor to accommodate tobacco chewers.

In 1863, the first public school in Pacific County was started in Oysterville. The Reverend John Dennison, a six-foot-two preacher, arrived in 1871. When he had an argument with a saloon keeper and the latter threatened to beat him up, the minister sent word to the saloon keeper "to come and try."

"Tell him I didn't grow six-feet-two for nothing," he was reported as saying. Dennison raised the money and built the Oysterville Methodist Church. It had a Catholic-type cross atop its belfry because Dennison had tackled a drunk for a donation.

The man, a good Catholic, agreed to support the construction, "if there would be a cross atop the church." Dennison accepted the offer. (This old Methodist Church was blown down in the 1921 hurricane.)

In 1891, two prisoners in the Oysterville conty jail, awaiting retrial, were shot by irate citizens who took the law into their own hands. ✂

Pinkney, a Ghost Town

All that's left of Pinkney City in eastern Washington State are the ghosts and the remains of the spring that supplied the once flourishing city with water.

Most of the land is now under cultivation, but in the 1860s, Pinkney City was a boom-town, with population of over 1,000. There were shootings, hangings, lynchings, court trials and organized posses. Saloons, hurdy-gurdies and box houses flourished and Pinkney City was a boisterous, busy place.

Pinkney City was on maps from 1859 to 1875 and at that time was the only city in the area around the present site of Spokane.

Fort Colville was next door and was probably the reason for Pinkney City achieving its size and its reputation. The fort was established in 1859 as a military post of the U.S. Army. (It was miles away from the 1825 Hudson Bay Company's Ft. Colville, a fur trading post beside Kettle Falls.) At the time of the establishment of the Army's Ft. Colville, there was Indian trouble in the country and four companies of the 9th U.S. infantry were stationed there.

The fort was under the direction of Major Pinkney Louiganbiel, and the civilians across the creek, being public relations minded, named their growing settlement for him.

The first buildings at the fort were hewn logs, and when the major couldn't buy sawed lumber at a reasonable price from the local mill, he built a dam two miles above the fort and put in a sawmill. After he had enough lumber for the fort, he leased the mill to civilians who then supplied cheap lumber to townsfolks and hastened the building of Pinkney City.

When the Civil War broke out, Pinkney was replaced by a

Major Curley who brought two companies of California volunteers to the fort. There were rumors that these men were San Francisco "jailbirds." Subsequently, there were numerous shootings and an increased amount of crime in Pinkney City, but the citizens feared the Indians more than they did the troops, and feared the Army would move the troops and abandon the post because of the Civil War which had broken out.

As late as 1871, a memorial was adopted by residents declaring that Stevens county (the area) was inhabited by Spokane, Coeur d'Alene, Isle de Pierre, San Poil, Okanogan and Lake Indians and only a "few" white settlers. The Indians were kept in check, the memorial stated, because of the presence of troops. When it was rumored that the troops were to be removed, the Indians became "emboldened and openly arrogant and announced their intention of driving the white settlers out and taking possession of their property.

"If the troops are removed, we will be unable to protect ourselves," the memorial declared.

In 1880, after the Army built Ft. Spokane, troops were withdrawn from Ft. Colville. Within a few years the fort land was appraised and sold, and the town of Pinkney completely disappeared. The county seat was moved to Spokane Falls.

To reach the site of Pinkney City and Ft. Colville, follow the secondary highway 3 miles northeast from Colville to Mill Creek. Here a flat valley extends over a mile. The area south of Mill Creek was the site of the fort. Across Mill Creek can be seen the site of Pinkney City. To the east of the road can still be seen flat places scooped out of the side of the hill where the pioneers placed their cabins and businesses.

❖

Parker Builds Palace

A grand house called "The Palace," with carved marble fireplaces, the finest English furniture brought around the Horn, and the Willamette Valley's first wall-to-wall carpet, was the social center for mid-Willamette Valley activities in the early 1850s.

The Palace was located at Parkersville, which was reached by Brown's Cow Path in early days and later by the "Skinny Pavement." Parkersville is just a ghostly memory of its former bustle now, but it was once a busy center and was even under consideration for a time as the capital of Oregon.

A man with a mysterious background, William Parker, was the moving force of Parkersville. He was born in England in 1814 and ran away from home at 14 and worked his passage to America. He never communicated with his family thereafter and never told anyone why he had left home.

Parker married in Illinois in 1841 and evidently contracted tuberculosis shortly thereafter. Five years later he came West, but there is no record of the trip. Settling just north of Silverton, the Parkers took a 640 acre donation land claim as provided by the Oregon Donation Land Grant, with 320 acres to the wife, "to be held in her own right."

The Willamette Valley's famous "Battle of the Abiqua River" with the Indians in 1848 involved Parker and after the Indians were subdued, Parker and a Loreza Byrd left for the California goldfields, where evidently they "struck it rich."

Returning home, the two men built a mill and a dam for water power to run it and Parkersville was born.

The dam washed out a couple of times, but Parker always

rebuilt it and his grist mill was such a success that Parkersville became a trading center for people from all over the Mid-Willamette Valley. Other businesses sprang up around the mill and the importance of Parkersville increased.

The Democratic County convention met there in 1859, and ambitious schemes were advanced to make Parkersville even more important. A post office had been established in 1852, and it was recognized that transportation was Parkersville's biggest problem. Parker and the politicians attempted to solve this problem by an ambitious scheme to make the Pudding River a navigable stream.

The Pudding River Transportation and Navigation Company was incorporated and was granted a charter by the Leigslature for "control of the river."

The center for all social life in Parkersville was "The Palace," the impressive home of the William Parkers. It also had another nickname, "The Hotel," because the stages all stopped there and many dignitaries and friends of the Parkers frequently stayed overnight.

Parker died unexpectedly in 1859 after contracting pneumonia, which evidently was complicated by his tuberculosis. His wife remarried twice, and the mills were sold in 1874.

After the sale of the mills and their final closure, the dams were destroyed and Lake Labish behind the dams was drained with the idea of leaving productive lake bottom soil.

Shortly afterward "The Palace" was torn down, the businesses vanished and Parkersville disappeared.

Portland Gets Bull Run

The man who is said to have first had the idea of bringing Bull Run water to Portland was a trapper named George Hodges, who was well acquainted with the area and its mountains, streams and rivers.

Sometime in the 1850's, A. B. Cunningham came to Portland, and after looking around declared that it was destined to become a big city but that its water supply was inadequate.

Cunningham sent for Hodges and asked him where there was an abundant supply of good water.

"I told him that Bull Run was as good as there was, so he hired me to go up to the headquarters and bring out a five-gallon demijohn for analysis," Hodges reported later.

Up until 1857, Portland had obtained its domestic water supply from a dam in the canyon west of 7th Street. Fir logs were bored by hand and served as pipes for the water. In 1865, water from two nearby creeks was added to the system, and in the late 1860's a pumping station was put in the Willamette River at the foot of Lincoln to pump water to the two new reservoirs at 4th and Market and 7th and Lincoln.

In the 1880's, another pumping station was added at Palatine Hill.

When the private water companies about town learned by rumor about the possibility of Bull Run water, they made attempts to thwart any such plans. Hawthorne Springs in East Portland, and Crystal Springs on the Ladd farm were suggested as other possible sources of municipal water supplies.

Another group began touting Sucker Lake near Oswego, and still another group suggested Johnson Creek and the

Clackamas River as nearer and more practical sources of water.

One enterprising water system owner, McGuire, who had the system at Hawthorne Springs, decided to file for water rights on every trickle of water between Bull Run and the Sandy River. He traveled by raft and it took him 20 days to make the rounds to tie up the rights and put notices on every stream and spring that he could find.

In the meantime, Cunningham and his partner, Talbot, hired a surveyor to survey Bull Run and the other streams, but the owners of the other water companies managed to get Hodges and two or three others to sign up as the surveyor's crew and they managed to keep the surveyor drunk as long as he was out on his project. When he got back, neither he nor anyone else could read his notes or make sense of his findings.

Eventually, the warring water factions conceded that Cunningham and Talbot had the edge on them with their Bull Run water and dropped out of the water race. The city analyzed the Bull Run water and spent several months taking record of flow. Finally, they bought the rights for Bull Run water from Cunningham and Talbot and began bringing water to Portland. The project required 300 miles of distributing mains, and $5 million had been spent on the Bull Run water system by 1910.

Olympia By-Passed

"Opportunists, planning "to make a million," probably were responsible for Washington State's capital city of Olympia being by-passed by the Northern Pacific Railroad when it built its tracks from Tacoma to Portland.

For a number of years, Olympia smarted because of the lack of train service and the city was threatened with loss of the state capital because many persons wanted to move the state govenrment to "someplace where rail and train service are adequate."

In the early days, Olympia had a shallow bay, with a long pier extending about half a mile to deep water. When plans for a railroad running along the sound from Tacoma south to Portland began, surveys were made and it was decided that the Olympia railroad terminal should be at the end of the pier at Main and First Streets, to provide access to the docks.

At this point, several men, seeing the the opportunity to do themselves good, organized the Priest Point Land Company and bought up all land planned for use as terminals of the railroad in Olympia. They succeeded in bottling up the site completely and announced they planned to make "a cool million on sale of the land."

A representative from their company was sent to St. Paul to negotiate with the Northern Pacific Company for purchase of the land, but no deals were forthcoming.

Then one morning, Olympia woke up to discover that the railroad had been built through the county fifteen miles east of Olympia. The Priest Point Land Company still owned the terminal sites along the bay.

A few years later, Olympia volunteers with wagons, picks

and shovels and lots of determination built a railroad from Olympia to Tenino to connect with the Northern Pacific line. However, train service "was not what the population demanded" and Olympia was threatened with loss of the state capital until 1909 when the present million dollar statehouse was finally authorized.

The Washington legislature had provided for the sale of 132,000 acres of capital lands and a statehouse had been started in 1890, but trouble followed. The question of legality arose and the contractor stopped work.

The panic of 1893 followed and for almost 20 years the foundation sat as a monument of capital frustration. Once again, when the legislature attempted to build a capitol, Governor John R. Rogers, Washington's "Barefoot Schoolboy" governor, vetoed the bill. Instead, he bought the white elephant Thurston Courthouse and remodeled it. This plan was makeshift and unsatisfactory and finally in 1909, authorization was given for the present capitol building and the question of removing the capital from Olympia was finally settled. ❖

Fire Department Drafted

The great Seattle Fire of 1889 inadvertently put the Seattle Fire Department in the garbage business for a number of years, and they didn't like it!

When the fire raged through the Seattle waterfront destroying wharves, as well as most of the rest of the town, the city council decided they had better have a fireboat.

The fireboat "Snoqualmie," later to be renamed the "Robert Eugene," was designed. It was 90 feet in length, with two boilers, and a compound steam engine.

Robert Moran shipyard in Seattle was the lowest bidder and in 1891 the fireboat was completed and was ready for duty. She was the pride of the Seattle Fire Department.

The only problem was that there were no waterfront fires for a long period of time and Seattle's frugal town fathers decided the fireboat could act as a tug and haul the garbage scow out to be dumped. (In those unenlightened times, the garbage was dumped in Puget Sound — far enough out that hopefully it didn't wash ashore near the city.)

The fire department was incensed, but for several years they dutifully hauled the garbage.

Two additional fireboats, "The Duwamish" in 1910, and the "Alki" in 1928 were added to the fleet and the "Robert Eugene" was finally sold for $1,888.

But the gallant 90-foot "Robert Eugene," the first fireboat, and the faithful garbage tug proved to be made of stern stuff. It was used as a workboat in the construction of the Lake Washington Floating Bridge in 1939, and today it is still a workboat on Puget Sound.

Heighth of luxury marked 1910 Sol Duc Resort and Spa in heart of Olympic Mountain rain forest. Hotel had 165 rooms and was hewn from huge Douglas fir timbers. Tastefully decorated rooms boasted telephones, hot mineral baths and steam heat, but visitors faced rugged trip to reach hot springs.

Hot Springs Popular

The Northwest once had one of the largest and most elegant health spas in the world.

Construction of this magnificent health resort which took advantage of the mineral waters of Sol Duc Hot Springs on the Olympic Peninsula was begun in 1910.

The four-story hotel with 165 bedrooms was constructed of massive upright hewn Douglas fir logs. Every modern convenience of the time was included, including hot and cold running water, telephones, private mineral baths and steam heat. All rooms had outside views of the surrounding rain forest and many rooms had private balconies.

Fredrick and Nelson's head interior decorator spared no expense in decorating the huge lobby and elegant dining room. There were gold trimmings on white backgrounds and brass chandeliers were used as the grand hotel's motif.

In addition, the resort sported a separate grand ballroom, gymnasium, power house, steam laundry and cabins. Most important was a sanatorium for the hopeful patients coming to be cured of rheumatism, liver disorders, diabetes, skin problems, blood disorders, alcoholism and tuberculosis.

This sanatorium was a 100-bed, 3-story facility with the most modern medical equipment of the time. It had x-ray, an operating room, laboratory and full time doctors and nurses who treated and cared for guests.

For those who just wanted to get away from it all, or just wanted to vacation, the trip to the remote resort, set in the wildest part of the wild Olympics, also offered complete recreation facilities, including a golf course, tennis courts, bowling alley and numerous swimming pools.

The most surprising thing about this amazingly luxurious

been to get to the place in the early 1900's. Even today, with modern transportation, it takes a special effort to get to Sol Duc Hot Springs, now a part of the Olympic National Park. In 1910, the trip was a real excursion.

Seattle, Washington was the closest city of sizeable population and was the usual launching point for the trip. From Seattle, it was necessary in 1910 to board a steamer at Coleman Dock and travel to Port Angeles, a distance of over 100 miles. Then there were almost 20 miles of primitive road to reach the edge of Lake Crescent. As there was no road around the lake at that time, it was necessary then to board another boat for a 12-mile ferry trip the length of the lake. From the point where the little ferry docked it was another 15 miles of rough roads to the Sol Duc Hot Springs Health Spa and Resort.

Yet, the fame of the place spread, and people came from all over the United States and the world and the resort flourished. Cost of the trip from Seattle was $11.00 and resort rates at the time were $3.00 per day. However, these were the days when many laborers were paid only $1.00 per day, so most of the clientele were the affluent or the desperate who sought medical cures from the mineral waters.

Many diseases were recognized at the time, but there were very few effective treatments so much faith was placed on the miracle cures of the mineral waters. More than 10,000 persons made the trip to Sol Duc Health Spa in 1915 hoping for better health.

Indian legend surrounding the hot springs 15 miles up the Sol Duc river had long attributed mythical power to the waters. Two dragons had engaged in a fierce battle here, according to the legend, but neither of the dragons could win and both remain shedding hot tears, which are the two hot springs.

Unfortunately, on May 26, 1916, sparks from the chimney ignited the cedar shake roof on the main Sol Duc hotel building. In three hours almost all the structures of the resort were burned to the ground. Over $300,000 worth of facilities wre destroyed, never to be rebuilt in their grandiose style.

Many years later, Fred Martin built the present Sol Duc Hot Springs Resort which consists of store, swimming pool and cabins.

In 1966, the United States government bought the resort for $880,000 and made it a part of the Olympic National Park. The hot pool and the adjacent camp grounds are still a popular, but remote vacation site.   ❖

Sol Duc Sanitarium was 100-bed medical facility with doctors and nurses to treat patients who came to take hot water cures.

HEALTHY MEDICINE ?

Horse and Buggy Medicine

The study and practice of medicine have changed a bit since Dr. D. M. Brower (1858-1939) graduated from medical school 94 years ago.

So . . . by way of a reminder, here are a few highlights from a paper he read to the Jackson County Medical Society in 1930.

In the spring of the year 1888, the professors and preceptors of Willamette University granted David Marcus Brower a diploma conferring upon him the degree of Doctor of Medicine.

Taking a raw country boy from the hills and sticks of Marion County, Oregon, whose education was in the ungraded public school, but with added reading and study, the officials decided to admit him.

In a few years, with very sparse and inefficient clinical material available in the hospitals of Portland making an M.D. was a grinding process and here's hoping it will not be repeated very often.

The hospitals were very unsanitary and inefficient and because of such conditions, gave such poor service in clinical teaching that attendance and observation disgusted our country boy, although he knows that hospitals now are far better.

Opening an office in Roseburg in the fall of 1888, things soon grew rosy. A successful coping with an epidemic of variola or smallpox that winter brought him into the limelight.

However, urged by a push and a pull he left it all, possibly because he could not stand prosperity, and went west to Myrtle Point, 65 miles west from Roseburg.

The memory of the four years of medical practice in and in the vicinity thereof, leaves a taste in the mouth, both bitter and sweet, bitter mostly. His thesis at the time of graduation was "Prophylaxis" — the recollection was a mockery as far application of its teaching was concerned. If such a thing as sanitation existed in or adjacent to Myrtle Point, it was never in evidence.

Diphtheria — Ah, would God that antitoxin had at the time been available. Many a defeat would have been turned into victory — many a child now dead, might be living.

Added to diphtheria and typhoid fever, came LaGrippe, or "Flu" — a name that by its use makes it possible to hide much of our ignorance as to what ails our patients from the laity — hit the West Coast in the winter of 1889-90.

Whole families went to the sick bed almost in one day. Added to the joys of the practitioner came the awful flood of said winter. Beginning the eighth of January, rain fell almost continuously for six weeks.

Practice of medicine, under such conditions, was no picnic. When the trail reached the river, getting in a row boat, and swimming your horse by the side of the boat to the opposite bank or shore was no small risk.

One of the saddest events of that awful winter occurred in a family that lived one and one half miles up the river from Myrtle Point. The mother of the family had lost her first husband, by whom she had six children, and a little son two years old, by her second husband. Her 13-year-old son, Trice, took gripal pneumonitis and soon two more of the children took the disease. By the time Trice began to convalesce, the worn-out mother took sick. Being in the third month of pregnancy — the end could be seen from the beginning. In a few days she miscarried and died.

The house was an open one and rain dashed in the windows and under the doors. The river rose until one could almost step from the boat to the door step. The dead woman was carried to the side of the sick children for the last look at their only parent. One could hardly live long enough to forget a scene like that.

Many a time in days past a trip to the grocery store for those in beggarly want was more indicated than one to the druggist. Often then and since, the psychology that followed a little help, accompanied by a cheery voice, a smile accompanied by a story told to cheer the patient gave her something to remember.

More especially was this true when quarantine meant cutting off all communication with outside people except the attending physician. No daily newspapers — no phone —no radio — nothing but long dreary days of loneliness with want in the offing.

The only change in the scenery was the coming of the attending physician, who would come in dressed in a rubber suit and high-topped rubber boots, but often was soaked to the skin because of a mis-step while wading a swift current. Coming in such a condition, but nevertheless bringing needed cheer may have required some effort, but it was worthwhile and for a wonder the patient would get well.

Consumption, or rather tuberculosis, in that damp, sunless climate and poorly ventilated dark rooms, with utter absence of sanitation, claimed many. Symptomatic treatment of such cases was the limit and always ended in a funeral.

Koch had isolated the tubercular bacilli, but knowledge to successfully combat the disease was lacking. The intelligent treatment and prevention that has arisen since is one of the marvels of the past two or three decades. In the days which we are describing, the ablest physicians when facing tuberculosis or cancer, bowed their heads and admitted defeat and departed, leaving no hope.

Another incident that occurred in his first year in Myrtle Point was almost a tragedy. Returning late one afternoon from down river in a row boat, he learned a man was badly hurt on the Middle Fork. The messenger had come by trail over Sugar Loaf Mountain, one of the highest in that part of the country, as the road around the mountain was closed by innumerable slides. Taking his large operating case and all he thought he needed, he hit the trail. He found a man with three badly broken ribs. The doctor had everything he needed but adhesive plaster.

He was eight miles from his base of supplies. It was dark, snow was falling on the mountains, no one could get back. They tried pine pitch to make a substitute plaster. It failed. He said, "Is there any black wax in this neighborhood." The reply was, "Yes, there are three balls of black wax upstairs." It was gotten pronto. Three strips of drilling were cut proper length and width. Quickly the wax was melted and spread. When cool enough, the improvised plasters were applied. Their application worked like magic — the patient getting immediate relief. Three weeks later the patient rode horseback into town, the plasters were removed, the ribs were as sound as on the other side.

Ashland was a very unsanitary town then. Diseases were engendered and spread by filth and poverty. The winter of 1894 an epidemic of Scarlet Fever spread over the town. After it got well scattered the Town Council appointed him as Chairman of the Health Board. Stoping the epidemic was some job, nevertheless by establishing an efficient quarantine and a campaign for sanitation there were no more new foci and the epidemic was stayed.

When the danger was on, the officers were very smooth and friendly, but when the danger was past and he presented his bill of $10.00, which ought to have been more than twice as much, his popularity waned promptly. Following the advice of the City Attorney, who was paid $50.00 per month, the Council allowed him $5.00 and fired him off the Board. Lesson: if you hold an office to serve the public, do nothing if you want to keep public approval.

During the 42 years that are past Hospitalization has appeared to harass the practitioner. The Pure Food and Drug Act cut into the Patent Medicine trade. Prohibition and the Volstead Act cut into the joys of the Medical Practitioner, causing some of us to complain bitterly and shout loud and long for the good old days of whiskey and castor oil.

The use of electricity, its light and heat used for healing, has all arisen in the past four years. The use of the vacuum cleaner has lessened calls for our services, like it or not.

Some may say, "Did you not make mistakes?" Yes, plenty, some serious. Unfortunately for me, I always had to admit it — a thing a doctor ought not to do. Somehow, I could not shift the responsibility to someone else — the nurse for instance.

Whether I live long or die soon, if I can truly be called "A Friend of Man" and have the approval of one who called himself the "Son of Man," I shall be satisfied.

Cabin Door Surgery

The back door of a forest ranger shack, taken off its hinges and set on two chairs became the operating table for an emergency appendectomy performed by Dr. Virgil C. Belknap who practiced in Oregon's John Day Valley in the 1890's.

Dr. Belknap was a true "horse and buggy doctor" and if he had to make a call where he couldn't get the buggy, he rode the horse. He came to Prairie City in 1894, and soon had the reputation of going on a call anytime, day or night. He also never worried about whether the people could pay, and he was said to be a fine surgeon.

When a call came from a forest ranger in the Long Creek area that his wife was very ill, Dr. Belknap set out promptly for the ranger's cabin. He found the wife had acute appendicitis and decided that she must be operated on at once. After the surgery, performed on the back-door operating table, Dr. Belknap stayed a day to make sure of her recovery.

Usually, he had two local women that he could call upon to administer anesthetic, and the kitchen or dining room table was frequently the operating surface for the doctor. Often he stayed with his patients until the crisis was over.

Amputations were frequent in those days when many persons in the John Day area worked in the mines, and the doctor was often up all night. Many times after a night session with sick patients, the doctor would be so tired that when he started for home, he would turn his horse loose, headed in the right direction, and would fall asleep in the buggy.

Dr. Belknap was highly regarded by everyone in the John Day Valley because in addition to his fine surgical reputation, and his medical skills, he was reported to have a very good sense of humor. He was also very civic minded and participated in community affairs.

On one occasion, he came to a masquerade party as the "Barefoot Boy with Cheeks of Tan." He always wore a goatee, or Van Dyke beard, but for this occasion he shaved it off, took off his glasses, wore bib overalls with the cuffs turned up. In addition, he was barefoot with his big toe bandaged in a rag.

Dr. Belknap was born in Benton County in 1871 and obtained his medical degree from Jefferson Medical College in Philadelphia.

Cookbook Cures

When the Northwest pioneers came west in their covered wagons; when they took the long treacherous voyage by ship around Cape Horn, or even when they came west on the first transcontinental railroad, medicine and medical care was pretty much a do-it-yourself proposition.

There were lots of opportunists who came along who called themselves "doctor," but were without qualifications, and there were lots of "sure cures" on the market; but most of these were simply varying potions of alcohol. Besides, the early settlers were often isolated on lonely homesteads or in small settlements far from outside help.

It is no wonder then that "folk medicine" was so important, and the 'bible' of medical help in those early days was usually the cookbook!

The prudent woman-of-the-house wouldn't think of starting west without a copy of one of the thick, early editions of The White House Cookbook or its early counterparts. Medical Hints from such an 1894 edition state that these "will save our readers many doctor's bills as well as much pain and suffering often, and possibly may even save a life."

Remember, these are not recommended procedures in view of today's more modern medical discoveries, but they were frequently practiced home medical treatment in the Northwest only a few years ago.

BOILS—Bind on a slice of ripe tomato; change frequently and burn the old slices. It affords speedy relief, is cool, soothing and hastens the cure.

BLACK EYE—Apply at once whiskey, brandy or spirits of wine. Never apply cold water, except a little at first, but appy a cloth wrung out of hot water — as hot as it can be borne.

COLIC—A teaspoon each of salt and finely pulverized black pepper in a glass of cold water will almost always give relief. Then give a dose of rhubard.

CORNS—Hard corns may be killed by binding on at night a piece of lemon, half a cranberry, or some cracker crumbs soaked in strong vinegar; leave on all night and pare off the corn in the morning.

CUTS and WOUNDS—The pain from common wounds may be quite speedily relieved by burning woolen cloth on a shovel of live coals and holding the injured part in the soke for 15 or 20 minutes. The smoke from common brown sugar burned on coals in the same way is also good.

DIARRHEA and DYSENTERY—Take ½ ounce tincture of rhubarb; ½ ounce spirits of camphor; ½ ounce of laudanum; ½ ounce peppermint; ½ ounce tincture of cayenne pepper and mix. Dose for an adult is 15-30 drops in a little water after each passage, according to age and the violence of the attack.

FATIGUE—Ladies who are tired from the labors of their housework will find marked relief if they will lie down for 5-10 minutes and spread over the face a cloth wrung out of hot water. It will brighten the eyes and smooth out the tired lines.

HEARTBURN—Take 5 grains of aromatic powder and 12 grains of bismuth; mix and give 3 times a day. It will almost alway give relief. Alkalies if given habitually will weaken the stomach. Those troubled with heartburn should drink sparingly at meals; avoid the use of fatty foods, pastry and the too exclusive use of vegetables.

HYSTERIA—Loosen the clothes and admit an abundance of fresh air; then hold the mouth and nose closed so as to stop the breathing for a short time. On releasing the hold, a long breath is at once drawn which usually results in relaxing the spasm and ending the fit.

HEADACHE—For nervous headaches and neuralgia, the following is an excellent remedy. Take a wide-mouth, glass stoppered bottle, half fill it with a soft sponge, and on this pour 3 drachms of a solution of bisulphide of carbon. Keep tightly closed. To use, remove the stopper and press the mouth of the bottle over the seat of pain for 5 minutes. Press tightly against the skin so that none of the vapor can escape. After 1 or 2 minutes, tingling is felt which in 3 or 4 minutes becomes rather severe, but it subsides at once when the bottle is removed. Any redness of the skin soon disappears.

HICCOUGH—Moisten either granulated or brown sugar with vinegar and eat it.

HIVES—Castor oil applied with the tips of the fingers to the pustules will give speedy relief to the itching. So will baking soda dissolved in warm, soft water. Then take 1 cup molasses, 1 tablespoon sulphur, 1 teaspoon cream of tartar and mix. Take 1 teaspoon each morning before breakfast until relieved.

NOSEBLEED—First, put the feet in water as hot as can be borne. This will usually stop it. Or pull up a piece of linen, saturate it with hamamelis or alum and stuff it up the nostril, or chew something shutting the jaws tightly together.

SLEEPLESSNESS—Take a sharp walk for about 20 minutes before retiring, or just before retiring sponge the surface of the body with very hot water, or take a cold bath followed by vigorous friction. These methods draw the blood to the extremities and away from the head, and so induce sleep. These plans are much better than using drugs.

SUFFOCATION—Remove patient at once to the fresh air; lay him on his back and loosen the clothing about his neck and chest. Dash cold water on the face and chest. Keep up the warmth of the body and apply mustard plasters over the heart and around the ankles. If these means fail, try artificial respiration as soon as possible.

Some of these "remedies" bring back memories which can be laughed about today, but probably your grandmother or your great-grandmother took them pretty seriously.

AROUND THE NORTHWEST

First Northwest Apples

Apples sold for $1 each in Portland in 1852!

Apple hungry pioneers snatched up the first Oregon grown apples from the Henderson Lewelling orchard in Milwaukie, and paid the high price without a grumble.

Lewelling had brought the young apple trees across the country, along with his wife and seven children, in a covered wagon in 1842. There were 700 small trees and shrubs planted in two specially constructed boxes built upon a wagon bed with 12 inches of dirt in them. A railing around the boxes guarded the trees from hungry cattle and horses during the trip.

Just before the Lewellings arrived in Oregon, an eigth child was born to Mrs. Lewelling. They named it Oregon Columbia Lewelling. Their trip from St. Joseph Missouri had taken six months and about half of the nursery stock survived the trip.

Landing in Milwaukie, the Lewellings bought five acres on the bank of the Willamette River and set to work clearing it so they could plant their trees. In March the next year, William Meek, also from Iowa, arived with some nursery stock in a box fastened to the tail gate of his wagon, and he and Lewelling decided to become partners in the nursery business. Meek bought adjacent land, and they began planting the apples, pears, quince, plum and cherry trees. These trees became the first grafted fruit trees on the Pacific Coast.

The nursery prospered from the first. Another Lewelling brother joined the partnership in 1850, and in 1851, the nursery advertised 20,000 apple trees for sale, along with 60 other varieties of fruit and berries.

Soon the Milwaukie orchard was supplying trees and

fruit to all of the Northwest and to the growing California market. By 1852, they were selling boxes of apples in Portland for as much as $75 and reported that four bushels of apples shipped to the California gold mines brought $500. In 1853, the Lewellings and Meek expanded and started branch nurseries in Salem and near Spring Valley, Oregon.

In 1856, Oregon exported about 20,000 boxes of apples to California, but by then Californians had seen the profit in fruit trees and had set out trees which they secured from the East. The result was that Oregon's fruit boom collapsed and fell so low that Meek moved to California in 1857, as did one of the Lewellings. Seth Lewelling and Joseph Lambert continued the Oregon orchards and became famous as propagators and developers of new and improved fruits.

Telephone Called Toy

In 1879 Olds and King had one of the most prosperous mercantile businesses in Portland. They were considered astute businessmen.

That was the year that ambitious J.H. Thather came to Portland as general manager of Western Union Telegraph company and he was determined to sell the idea of the company's new phone system to all Portland businesses.

When Thather approached Olds and King and asked them to subscribe to telephone service at $5 per month, he got a flat "No."

"We have no time to waste during business hours with a telephone," King told him. "It is a toy, and will never be important to businesses."

At the time, there were only 12 subscribers in the Portland area, and perhaps Olds and King were right in believing that it was best to send a messenger if you had anything to tell someone. After all, messenger boys could be hired at the time for about $5 per month, and could sweep floors in their spare time!

"Mr. Olds told me that he would bet any amount of money that I would bet that as long as they were in business, they would never install a telephone," Thather recalled later.

Thather remembered that he worked very hard those first years to increase the list of telephone subscribers, but that "I had to stand more abuse, good-natured raillery, jeers and even insults that first year than I ever had to afterward."

Thather remembered that Judge Bellinger had a telephone over on Portland's east side, and that he was one of the subscribers who often felt that the telephone was an annoyance with good reason.

"Everytime there was a fire anywhere within half a mile of his place at night time, *The Oregonian* would call him up and ask him to go see whose house or barn was burning, how it caught fire, and how much damage was done," Thather said.

Thather himself lived at Second and Hall Streets. He said he also had to get up at all hours of the night to accommodate neighbors who wanted to use his phone to call a doctor or to talk to some friends. He added that in those days it was considered unneighborly if a person having a telephone would not accommodate anyone within a dozen blocks who wanted to use it.

Thather recalls also that he used to have "considerable trouble" with several Portland residents who believed in what he called "muscular Christianity."

"If the operator did not give these subscribers immediate and courteous service, it was up to the operator to take to the tall timber," Thather remembered.

One customer came to the telephone office and "licked" the boy operator. Asked what the trouble was, he declared the boy was impudent. "When I asked for a number, he told me the line was busy, so I came down here and gave him a good thrashing to teach him better manners," the irate customer told Thather.

By 1882, the number of telephone subscribers in Portland had increased to 190, and they were still paying $5 a month. The year after that the number of subscribers increased to 500, and "Willie" Olds sent a messenger boy to the telephone office saying they had finally decided to install a 'phone at Olds and King Department Store!'

Horton Gets Hot Seat

One of the funny stories told for years about Dexter Horton, Seattle banker and one of the founding fathers of Seattle, was about the day he got the hot seat!

Horton was on his way downtown one raw morning when he decided to stop by a smouldering stump along the way and lift his coattails to warm himself.

Moments later he found himself sent sprawling with his pants half blown off and an embarrassing, but not dangerous, wound in his backside.

The stump had contained an old cannon ball from the warship Decatur during the short-lived war with the Indians a few years before. The powder charge had chosen that moment to explode when horton stopped to get warm. ❖

Outdoing Boston

By the 1880s, the frontier cities of the Northwest had developed a social caste system along with lavish living, social graces and Victorian behavior that made it hard to imagine that they had been settled for only about a generation.

In Portland, particularly, there were a number of nouveau riche who took pride in emulating Boston behavior to the extent that they almost outdid Boston. Great fortunes had been amassed during the early period, and since there was no aristocracy with a tradition, social standing was based almost entirely on wealth.

In appearance, the city itself still looked like a frontier town. Saloons still outnumbered other business establishments. Wooden Indians stood in front of cigar stores, and patent-medicine men still attracted crowds on street corners.

But some of the city's houses were the last word in elegance, like the Portland mansion with a hall lined with red leather and a forty-foot drawing room with marble mantles and floor-to-ceiling mirrors lining the walls at each end. The floor had a white velvet carpet decorated with bunches of roses. Another home of the time had a top floor ballroom for dancing and theatricals, complete with gas footlights.

Social events and balls were gay events with floating, beruffled skirts and the rustle of silks and satins. Gentlemen wore white kid gloves and wore boutonnieres in their lapels. It was a time of extravagance. Imported clothes were the style, and formal affairs were the vogue.

Manners were as formal as the dinners and the chaperoned balls. A lady kept both feet on the floor with one slightly in front of the other and never dared cross her knees. Using a first name was considered an act of intimacy, and some women never quite got used to addressing their husbands except as "Mr."

As in the East, Northwest "society" strove to be a part of the sentimental age of grandeur. The "Gay Nineties" moved the area into the time of the Gibson Girl, and behavior became a little more relaxed. Women took to the tennis courts and went cycling in starched shirtwaists and leather boots laced to the knees. Men wore straw hats, striped blazers and knickerbockers.

Sunbonnet Saved

A treasured sunbonnet was almost the undoing of 9-year-old Phoebe Crosby, an early-day relative of Bing Crosby's, who came to the Pacific Northwest with her family in the early 1850's.

In 1846, the United States sent Capt. Nathaniel Crosby, a sea captain, to take supplies to relieve the distress of immigrants who had joined the wild rush to seek their fortune on the Pacific Coast. The captain was so impressed with the possibilities of fortune to be gained here that he sent his elder brother back to bring the rest of the Crosby family west.

Because they were seafarers, the brothers bought a ship and loaded it up with family members and their possessions. They arrived on the West Coast at Portland in early 1850. Part of the family stayed in Portland, and part of the family went to Tumwater, Washington, to settle.

When the Indian war broke out, the Tumwater Crosbys were living on a farm several miles from where the settlers had built a blockhouse for protection from the Indians. One day some friendly Indians came to warn Crosby that there was danger of attack from hostile Indians. Crosby was skeptical that there was any real danger and decided to stay on the farm with his family, but the Indians told him to watch for signs of burning buildings.

And sure enough, that night, as soon as it was dark, the skies were lighted with flames of neighbors' barns set afire by enemy Indians.

The flames were convincing proof that the Indians were sincere in their alarm. Hastily arousing the children and dressing them, the family fled to the blockhouse.

In the haste and excitement of escaping, 9-year-old Phoebe's brand new subonnnet was left hanging on the kitchen wall.

After the family reached the fort, and while the parents were busy getting the young children settled for the remainder of the night, Phoebe slipped out into the dark and ran alone all the way back to her home to get her precious sunbonnet.

She returned safely, but many years later, she still remembered that she was severely reprimanded for her impulsive rescue of her sunbonnet.

Oregon Goose State?

In 1913, a battle was raging in the Oregon papers about an appropriate nickname for Oregon.

"Webfoot" was suggested by some, but others said it was an appellation, intended as burlesque and certainly was "misleading."

"Diversity" was expounded by some as being a perfect nickname, since Oregon had so many diverse industries and activities.

"Goose" was suggested, but wasn't too popular a name. Opponents said the goose was an emblem of stupidity and was a reflection on the industry and intelligence of the people of Oregon.

"Beaver," which finally won the nomination, was not popular with everyone. Some said the beaver indicated great industry and intelligence, but others said it was "misleading at this time because the beaver is nearly extinct," and therefore, the name was unfitting.   ❖